ADVANCE

"Rising levels of life expectancy and lite
and disease make this objectively one of the best times to be alive — we have
never had it so good. Yet at the individual level, many seem to have lost
touch with what it takes to make us happy. This book unpacks the recipe
for happiness, to best leverage our unique qualities in an increasingly AI
world. It gives the reader a valuable yet simple toolkit for building good
habits and getting rid of bad habits, in pursuit of wellbeing."

Dr. Liz Mellon, Chair of Editorial Board, *Dialogue,*
Duke Corporate Education

"Good health is a critical factor for the performance of our footballers,
basketball players and other sportsmen and women. Yet wellbeing is what
distinguishes the good teams from the great. We are continually engaged
with our athletes to give them the best chance of thriving in a highly
pressured environment and I see many parallels with what MacGregor and
Simpson have brought together for the business world. This is a timely and
indispensable guide for health, wellbeing and performance in today's world."

Dr. Gil Rodas, Medical Doctor, FC Barcelona

"If you care about improving your own wellbeing and that of your people,
this is the book for you! Steven MacGregor and Rory Simpson present a
bold vision and practical ideas for increasing the ROI of wellbeing into
every organization."

Professor Gretchen Spreitzer, Professor of Management
and Organizations, Michigan Ross School of Business

"In a world that will change beyond recognition in the next decade,
it is those people, and organizations who remember and embrace their
humanity who will best manage the inevitable turbulence. MacGregor
and Simpson provide that means of reconnecting with our human
selves and make an important contribution to the human awakening
so critical for our increasingly noisy world."

Pablo Rodríguez, CEO, Alpha

"Disruption is here, now, everywhere. Learning is the only way forward.
Chief Wellbeing Officer offers unique insights, entertaining thoughts,
and crazy ideas for survival and success in our new paradigm. In fact,
these guys are true paradigm pioneers."

Bernardo Quinn, CEO, Telefónica Latin America South

Published by
LID Publishing Limited
The Record Hall, Studio 204,
16-16a Baldwins Gardens,
London EC1N 7RJ, UK

524 Broadway, 11th Floor, Suite 08-120,
New York, NY 10012, US

info@lidpublishing.com
www.lidpublishing.com

A member of:
Business Publishers Roundtable.com

Printed in Spain by Cofás, S.A.

ISBN: 978-1-911498-77-3
Cover design: Juan Ramón Batista
Typesetting: produccioneditorial.com

First edition: June 2018

Steven P. MacGregor
& Rory Simpson

Chief ♥ Wellbeing Officer

LONDON   MONTERREY
MADRID   SHANGHAI
MEXICO CITY BOGOTA
NEW YORK   BUENOS AIRES

To the two Hughs, for making us who we are

CONTENTS

ACKNOWLEDGEMENTS

This book finally came together during the month of August, 2017. Between us, we travelled to Forres, Farletter, Findhorn, Orkney, Skye, Motherwell, Barcelona, Guatemala, Panama, The Andes, and even Easter Island. These unique places reminded us where we come from and where we are going. The people we interacted with, either as our executive students, friends, colleagues, or casual acquaintances along the way, are as much part of the story, as anything else.

As ever, the geographical journey is made memorable by the relational one. Our sincere thanks to Gordon Hush and all the team at the Highlands and Islands creative campus of the Glasgow School of Art, as well as all the team at Soho House Barcelona, for providing an inspiring writing base, and for Sonia Alvarez for keeping the sanity, and wine flowing, in Vallvidrera.

Our own thoughts have been made substantially richer by great conversations with those who very generously gave us their time, including Julie Cook, Ann Pickering, Roberto di Bernardini, Simon Pickard, Elsa Belugou, Ralf Buechsenschuss, Claire Hallmey, Aisling Campbell, Gretchen Spreitzer, Scott de Rue, Chris Barnes, Francesca Mastrogiacomi, Rubén Galcerán, Glenn Masterton, Ian Morrison, Aki Soudunsaari, Katherine Semler, Bernardo Quinn, Pilar Giron, Judith Janssen, Miguel Gowland, John Erceg, Greg Lee, David Falk, Brian McCarthy, Pablo Rodriguez and Myrtle, Robin, Rona, and Bruce Simpson.

Thank-you to Jeanne Bracken at LID for her belief and guidance in this project from the very beginning and her team for bringing our vision to life. To Ferran Bruguera for his hard work and creative talent in producing all figures for the book, many thanks.

And a final note to our loving and patient families. Matthew, Pamela, Harry, Pau, Jasmine and Lily: you make it all worthwhile!

TAKE-OFF
Welcome aboard

This book is for anyone who wants to create a more human workplace. *Chief Wellbeing Officer* is a comprehensive and accessible guide for enterprises of all shapes and sizes to improve health, happiness, and to achieve high performance. In an age where everyone is focused on digital transformation and artificial intelligence, the organizations that will thrive are those that increase their care for humans. In fact, the goal is a more human organization.

Our vision is to help create environments that allow leadership to flourish at all levels and functions of a business, in order to make the best of the many opportunities in this exciting age. It will be of particular interest to chief human resource officers, especially as they become more involved in the strategic direction of the company. Indeed, all managers in human resources, and learning and development, will gain value in an age where talent attraction and retention is a key differentiator, and where learning is a lifelong on-demand process.

We also see great value in this book for those outside of management. We hope to be of particular use to those charged with wellbeing in an organization at a relatively junior level, and that the discourse here may help them make the case for a louder voice. In a world where rapid change is the norm, leadership by example, and from all levels of the organization, is very much sought after. The holistic approach offered in *Chief Wellbeing Officer* will give any workplace professional the means to think about their own life and how that fits with work. Being able to reflect on and change behaviour can reap tremendous benefits through significant improvements in wellbeing.

Why Chief Wellbeing Officer?

The founder and executive chairman of the World Economic Forum, Klaus Schwab, wrote about the Fourth Industrial Revolution in 2016,[1] saying: "We stand on the brink of a technological revolution that will fundamentally alter the way we live, work, and relate to one another. In its scale, scope, and complexity, the transformation will be unlike anything humankind has experienced before." We see much of the present focus on the 'technological revolution', and present *Chief Wellbeing Officer* as the human side of 'living, working, and relating to each other'. Will a societal model emerge that allows our human selves to thrive in the new industrial age? Absolutely. Yet much pain may be endured to get there. As with any competitive context, those who are proactive in seeking the change and asking those tough questions will get ahead. And, for us, getting ahead means greater wellbeing at work, with all the benefits that brings.

We have worked with tens of thousands of executives throughout our careers, and believe that we are *all* executives now, irrespective of actual job title. Becoming more human at work is, in our view, critical to realizing the executive role that will increasingly be required of any professional.

What does 'executive' really mean? Let's consider the verb instead of the noun. Specifically the term *executive function* – those cognitive tasks carried out in the main by the frontal lobe part of the brain, and which include creative thinking, planning, strategizing, and judging. Such tasks are of course critical to all human beings, whether or not they are senior business leaders, with a key stage of infant development being linked to the development of executive function. Yet such tasks need to be of special interest to today's professional.

This is because the efficacy of executive function tasks has a close link to health. Research has shown that sleep deprivation does not significantly affect routine thinking, but does have a great impact on non-routine executive thinking. Exercise has also been shown to specifically benefit the frontal lobe part of the brain charged with executive function tasks. Such benefits dissipate after a few days, however, showing the need to continually invest in exercise as a busy business leader.[2]

So how should we action such knowledge in business? Of course we can try and change our own behaviour, yet the greatest impact may come from trying to implement such an approach in the leadership of our teams. Being an executive will almost always mean influencing and directing others – in many instances a great number of others. If in such leadership activity we include notions of health and wellbeing, we can transform the performance of those teams.

A future in which artificial intelligence (AI) plays an ever-deeper role in work and society will need more of our executive selves. And we need not adhere to the prophets of doom such as Elon Musk, who believes AI is the single biggest existential threat to the human race. The doomsday future scenario is supported by research, including an Oxford University study published in 2013 which found 47% of jobs in America to be at high risk of being "substituted by computer capital" soon.[3]

Another future scenario does exist – one in which the real danger may not lie in robots taking our jobs. Most cases of technology disruption show net job creation instead of job destruction such as the banking industry which we discuss later in the book.

Many observers feel the biggest impact of AI, at least in the short- to medium-term, will be the requirement for people to gain new skills to complement the new technology, and carry out those roles that AI cannot yet do. Highly empathetic jobs certainly. And, more generally, non-routine work. Essentially, a greater emphasis on executive function tasks each and every day. People can be better at their jobs with the technology of today and tomorrow, rather than fearing that their human skills will be devalued.

In an increasingly technological, digital, always-on world, it seems that the human factor will still be critical after all. And health and wellbeing will likely be an ever-greater driver of executive function. So we are all executives today. And tomorrow we'll need to be even more so.

The Fourth Industrial Revolution often focuses on the massive impact to come for business, government, and society at large. People are of course at the heart of all of these things, yet thinking also on the discrete, individual, human level is often missing. There are signs, thankfully, that caring for people is rising to the top of the agenda. Whether motivated by the need for better talent management or thinking about future ways of working, the best companies are giving their chief human resources officers a bigger say at board level, with some new titles representative of a shift in mindset.

The chief people officer term is becoming more and more common, albeit in the main for smaller start-up companies, and Apple announced in July 2017 a new vice president of people. Reporting directly to Apple CEO Tim Cook, Deirdre O'Brien will have responsibility for talent development, recruiting, benefits, compensation, and business support, as well as overseeing Apple University.

Would we like to see a more formal take-up of the Chief Wellbeing Officer role in business? Absolutely. Yet it is not our only aim. We see the beliefs and tools that comprise this book as being assimilated by people across the business. Is wellbeing a necessary term? We think it is, and prefer it to wellness, which is sometimes used instead, believing it to highlight a greater connection to human being, and to be a broader, more serious term, especially for business. The fantastic UK-based think tank Do Lectures nicely sums up the rationale as follows:[4]

> "A company has someone to look after money, strategy, and marketing etc. But soon there will be another title. A Chief Wellbeing Officer to look after humans. To create a culture that stops burnout, to create a culture of learning, to create a culture of thinking long-term. To put people before anything else. The pioneers already have them. They may call them another name, but they are one step ahead."

Happiness is a theme we introduced earlier and one we will return to later in the book. Chief Happiness Officer is another term that has surfaced in 2017. Some companies have created this new position as a result of a closer look at employee engagement and experience in recent years, while a range of recent global surveys seem to support the term, including Jones Lang Lasalle which found that 87% of people want such a position in their workplace.[5] We're open-minded. Our main intention isn't to argue vehemently for Chief Wellbeing Officer as the global standard, rather to put forward the vision of what that term represents. Though 'happiness' as a term seems to include many notions that will be covered in this book – including workplace design, which is a current area of focus for large real-estate consultants such as Jones Lang Lasalle, CBRE, and ISS – we're not sure it is a serious enough business term to be adopted in the long-run. Time will tell.

Structure of the book

The book contains three parts, moving from presenting the big picture towards concrete action. Part one is 'Chief', which highlights the top-level view of wellbeing, and discusses the key organizational and societal issues for more humanity at work.

Responsibility and purpose are key themes in discussing the role of business in society today and into the future. This first part of the book will set the foundations by focusing on the WHY, allowing us to address any cynicism over the presence of wellbeing at the top table of business.

We set the scene in chapter one through 'The Best Time to be Alive', an overview of our present age, and a quick look back at history and forwards to the future. Health and happiness, key themes throughout the book, are introduced. In 'The Fourth Industrial Revolution' we dig deeper on this critical inflection point in human history, considering our technology-driven future world and areas from death to education. Chapter three on 'Restoring Humanity to Leadership' reminds us that leadership is about other people, and details the purpose, values, and vision that may guide one's own life and that of others. The fourth and final chapter of part one, 'The ROI of Wellbeing', turns towards the business case, looking at how progress is measured in business and society, and some of the strategies currently being developed by leading organizations around the world.

Part two of *Chief Wellbeing Officer* is 'Wellbeing' and focuses on the WHAT. We look more closely at human nature, which sets the template for what the future of work must look like.

We start with two chapters developing the idea of total intelligence, something that has guided much of our own work over the past ten years and has helped develop thousands of executives around the world. Chapter five, 'Leading Through Emotional Intelligence' focuses on the emotional part of intelligence, again developing the human dimension of leadership introduced in chapter three. The following chapter six, 'Leading Through Physical Intelligence', looks in greater depth at our physical selves and the importance of considering leadership, of both ourselves and others, from an athlete's point of view. Learning is a key part of wellbeing today and 'Learning to Live' considers the life-long need for learning, and how S-curves, a concept first developed to look at technological change and innovation, can help us navigate through the rollercoaster of our longer lives. Navigating highs and lows is an area that continues in the final chapter of part two, 'A Day in the Life', where we look at our daily rhythms. We take a chrono-biological look at our current ways of working and how future patterns of work in a technologically-driven, always-on world will depend even more on these natural rhythms.

The third and final part of the book is 'Officer' and is the HOW of ownership and implementation. We aim to highlight good organizational practice and provide guidance for the reader on the myriad challenges and opportunities presented in the book. It is the prescriptive part of our discourse, but we try and detail the right questions for you, as opposed to thinking we have all the answers.

Chapter nine, on 'Design for Wellbeing', discusses how a design-thinking approach may be useful in implementing a more human-based workplace. Design is, above all things, human and key design skills may be used to guide a different type of daily leadership activity. In 'The Seven Hacks of Highly Effective Habits' we detail the seven elements that need to be considered to sustainably change behaviour in the workplace. Much has been written in recent years about the habits that are required for success on a personal or professional level, but much less exists on how such habits may be implemented. In chapter 11, 'Environmental Design', we focus on two of these elements to show how we may build the optimum workplace environment. In a digital world, a detailed look at the physical environment matters more than ever, and needs to be complemented by a similar approach to the social environment. In the 12th and final chapter, 'Leading in the Fourth Industrial Revolution' we bring our discussion to a close by reflecting on the main points of the book, summarising the key leadership attributes needed to fully realize the vision of Chief Wellbeing Officer. We hope it is a strong call to action to make your own contribution to that vision.

Let's get started.

PART 1

CHIEF

Starting with the WHY of *Chief Wellbeing Officer*, we look at the working world around us today and establish the human foundations upon which a more enlightened approach to leadership may rest_____

1

THE BEST TIME TO BE ALIVE

"Are you telling me that you built a time machine... out of a DeLorean?"

Marty McFly, *Back to the Future*

IN A CITY that is both *mar* and *muntanya* (sea and mountain) Barcelona has no shortage of stairs. There is, however, a set that is less well-known. This secret stairway winds itself up from the upper part of the Sarrià neighbourhood, starting at the world-renowned Montserrat school and delivers you into the main square of the village of Vallvidrera. Now, if you were to climb these 477 steps you would surely be tired but happy to enjoy the best views of the city of Barcelona.

Let's say you devise a strategy to make those 477 steps a little less daunting. Good practice in fields such as learning or athletic training would advocate breaking a big goal down into bite-size chunks. Maybe taking 40 steps at a time then pausing for breath would seem a reasonable approach. So where do those 40 steps take you? A little less than 10% of the way to enjoying those fabulous views (and perhaps a well-deserved refreshment in the town square), right? What if we change the scale? Do you know where 40 steps would take you if we substituted the linear scale for an exponential one? The moon!

We present this vignette as a way of understanding the shift in mindset that is happening today in many areas of society, from technology advance to population increase. Many people believe we are at a tipping point in human history, with an artificial intelligence-driven near-future ready to bring about unprecedented levels of change.

Arriving at the moon is an appropriate image, with 'moonshot thinking' being increasingly employed by ambitious, innovative, and disruptive organizations worldwide. First coined by Google X in 2010 (now simply X after the group name change to Alphabet in 2015) moonshot thinking is inspired by the original moon landing in 1969 – an incredibly difficult thing to do, with little actual understanding at the time of setting the goal of how to actually do it. Aiming for the impossible and starting from scratch are therefore two of the defining factors of moonshot thinking. The combination of *"a huge problem, a radical solution to that problem, and the breakthrough technology that just might make that solution possible"* is, according to X, the essence of a moonshot.

Though pioneered by a business, much of the focus is on grand challenges that face society as a whole. Examples within the X portfolio include Waymo, the self-driving car, and Project Loon, which aims to bring the internet to the most inaccessible parts of the world via hot-air balloons. Projects 'graduate' when they are mature enough to be developed within another part of the business, including Google Brain, which is driving development in artificial intelligence.

Aiming for the impossible and starting from scratch are therefore two of the defining factors of moonshot thinking.

The change in thinking where failure is celebrated (even encouraged) and short-term value is eschewed in favour of the deep learning that drives long-term leaps needs a supportive environment, of course. It also needs people who have a deep passion for what they are doing on a day-to-day basis. Will we be able to create a critical mass of these passionate, supportive environments to truly realize a shift to exponential progress?

Tim Urban covers many of the key points related to the changes likely to be driven by artificial intelligence on his popular Wait But Why blog.[1] He presents an accessible and amusing overview of AI, introducing concepts such as the Law of Accelerating Returns developed by the futurist Ray Kurzweil. In a nutshell, the next 30 years will return a far greater level of progress than the previous 30 years, and so on. As an example, Kurzweil suggests that the progress of the entire 20th century would have been achieved in just 20 years at the rate of advancement experienced in the year 2000.

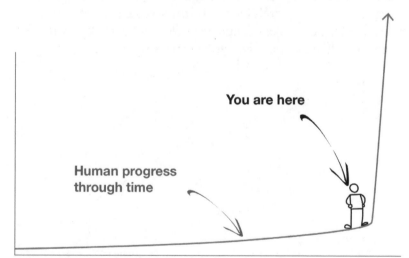

Figure 1.1. Human progress through time, adapted from *The AI Revolution: The Road to Superintelligence* by Tim Urban

Why is it so difficult to fully absorb the difference between linear and exponential progress? After all, the concept of exponential growth as related to the internet age has been gaining momentum for several years – ex-Google CEO Eric Schmidt said in 2010 that "we create as much data in two years as we did from the dawn of civilization up to 2003", yet it remains a difficult concept to grasp. More recent commentary, such as 'what happens in an internet minute', often takes on the numbers-heavy tone of world economics that results in most of us simply glazing over.

Getting to the moon through 40 exponential steps may allow a greater impact of the scale of change to hit home. A possible explanation for the general difficulty may be appreciated in the figure below, which helped frame Urban's analysis. Simply put, we can't see into the future. And the near future, according to Urban and many other AI commentators, is likely to yield significant advance due to the current status of computing power. Today, a $1,000 machine has around the equivalent processing power of a mouse (around 1/1000 of a human brain), yet continuing this trajectory using Moore's Law and other accepted historical trends will yield the equivalent of human intelligence by 2025 – with the sum of all human brains on Earth to follow soon after.

Figure 1.2. Human progress to the present day, adapted from *The AI Revolution: The Road to Superintelligence* by Tim Urban

We wanted flying cars, instead we got 140 characters.

Not everyone agrees that this line is about to dramatically kick-up. When we arrived at 21 October 2015, the date at which Marty McFly was shown to arrive in *Back to the Future Part II,* there was a societal shrug of the shoulders and a palpable sense of disappointment.

On more careful reflection, 21 October 2015 did indeed have an abundance of innovation and progress in comparison to 1989, when the sequel was originally released. Many of the future ideas, including virtual-reality movies, roll-up TV screens, and drones do exist in some form today, while the really big ideas, such as flying cars, may not be as far off as we think, given the rapid development of drone technology and the start of services such as drone-powered flying taxis in Dubai. In general, it's hard to be too critical when we consider that the World Wide Web only came into existence the same year the film was released, with the first web browser not coming until the following year.

Nevertheless, dissenting, disappointed, and underwhelmed voices exist. PayPal co-founder Peter Thiel wrote in 2010[2] that the technology industry had let people down, saying that "we wanted flying cars, instead we got 140 characters" (in a clear reference to Twitter).

Taking a more optimistic stance in his role as guest editor in the November 2016 issue of *Wired* magazine, Barack Obama said that now is the best time to be alive. The core message of Obama's editorial is people coming together to achieve big things. In spite of the undoubted progress that underpins his principal statement, he notes with optimism the great challenges that lie ahead, including climate change, economic inequality, cyber-security, terrorism, and cancer. The final months of his administration in Autumn 2016 also included the formation of a taskforce to tackle a Cancer Moonshot.

Part of the inherent logic in Obama's statement is that any present date is the best time to be alive, precisely because of the progress we make as a human race. So tomorrow, next week, and next year should be viewed as the best times to be alive respectively. Apart from being a boon to mindfulness advocates worldwide, the predictions of our move to more exponential progress should see the relatively near future as providing ever greater appeal, provided we adopt the right mindset to deal with massive change; change, of course, not being the most palatable concept for most of us.

Healthier than ever before, and happier?

There is no doubt we are progressing as a human race. Even for the most fervent sceptic of the modern world, all the data points to now being the best time to be alive. Though some argue that we are not moving fast enough, many of the major global development goals, with the exception of income inequality, are going in the right direction. Extreme poverty is decreasing around the world, average life expectancy will soon hit 90 years in certain developed countries, and people including Bill Gates – given the significant strides made by the Gates Foundation – hail the achievement of major milestones such as the virtual eradication of polio.

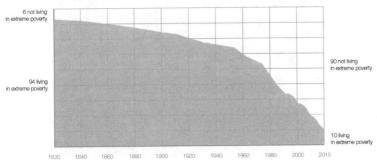

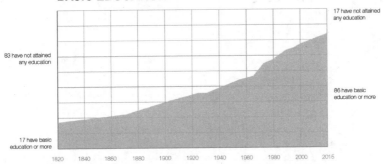

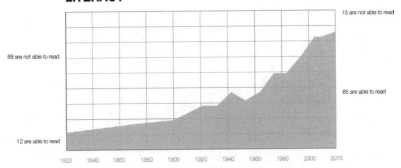

Figure 1.3. The world as 100 people in poverty, education and literacy the past 200 years, adapted from *Our World in Data* by Max Roser (ourworldindata.org)

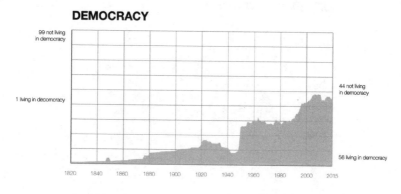

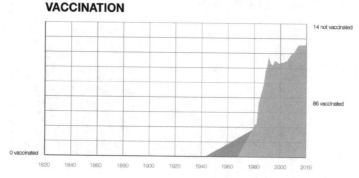

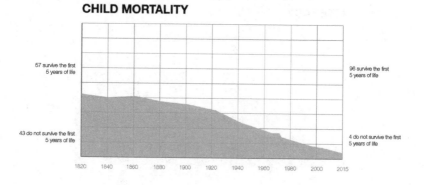

Figure 1.4. The world as 100 people in democracy, vaccination and child mortality the past 200 years, adapted from *Our World in Data* by Max Roser (ourworldindata.org)

So levels of health, wellbeing and prosperity are unmatched in human history. Yet are we really happier than ever before? The first World Happiness Report by the United Nations was released in 2012. Since then the UN believes there to be increasing evidence of happiness being considered the proper measure of social progress and the goal of public policy – something we look closer at in chapter four. Norway tops the happiness rankings in the latest report,[3] while also experiencing a significant drop in oil prices. Note is made that the country "chooses to produce its oil slowly, and invests the proceeds for the future rather than spending them in the present". The other countries in the top four – Denmark, Iceland and Switzerland – rank highly on all the main factors found to support happiness: care, freedom, generosity, honesty, health, income, and good governance. Other highlights which link to some of our points in this chapter include the fact that China is no happier than 25 years ago, while happiness in the United States continues to decrease from a high of ten years ago.

We look in greater detail at the concept of happiness in the workplace in chapter four. On a basic level we think most would agree that the working world today is characterized by a work-life balance that is increasingly out of kilter, while levels of work-related stress and poor health are on the increase. People complain about being overworked and plagued by 'busy-ness'; and happiness, at least for the professional class, remains as elusive a concept as ever. Does the happiness strategy being promoted by the Government of Dubai point towards a future wellbeing society, or does it merely support the thrill-seeking stereotype of the Gulf hub? In sum, more people are working than ever before, but more people are workaholics.

The materialistic and capitalistic drive to accumulate more things, more money, and more of everything is destroying our happiness. How did we let this happen? When did we lose

When did we lose our understanding of what actually brings us fulfilment, serenity, and peace?

our understanding of what actually brings us fulfilment, serenity, and peace? After the devastation of World War II the world was in survival mode. Everybody was driven by a need to recover, rebuild, and restart. This necessity gave people a purpose and the Western World, at least, was happier than it had ever been. Once societies were back on their feet, and disposable incomes were higher than ever, instead of pausing to appreciate the wealth and the success, we careered off course. We took the wrong road. Money, money, and more money somehow became the only goal, the only pursuit, the only valid measure of success. In the long-run this addiction could destroy us individually and also as a planet. The excesses of demand, and the subsequent cost to the environment could be our downfall. Over the last 50 years, per-capita incomes in developed countries have increased several-fold, and the increase in average happiness within these countries has been zero.

We recognize the need for security and betterment in one's life. We have witnessed poverty and how the lack of money can have a detrimental effect on the quality of life. Our home country Scotland, while being a well-functioning and generally prosperous country, is not an affluent one. Many wellbeing programmes at companies now include financial wellbeing, a dimension of one's life that can cause significant stress if not managed correctly. The economists Daniel Kahneman and Angus Deaton looked at the correlation between happiness and income for a sample in the United States.[4] They looked at two measures of happiness, day-to-day emotional wellbeing (how are you feeling today?) and life evaluation (looking back on your life, how satisfied are you?). Day-to-day happiness increased up to an income of $75,000, after which it topped out. They concluded that: "High income buys life satisfaction but not happiness, and that low income is associated both with low life evaluation and low emotional wellbeing."

We've seen that the evidence for day-to-day happiness and wellbeing are completely unrelated to financial status. We spend a significant amount of time teaching in Latin America. In any country that is significantly poorer than anywhere in Western Europe what impacts us greatly is how happy the people are. They choose to be happy. If you open your eyes and observe street market sellers, passers-by, people just sitting around – all mostly seem happy. We then fly back to Europe and see the crowds in the luxury duty-free shops, with all of their wealth and not a single smile anywhere! Have we replaced happiness with the pursuit of wealth?

The good news is that the solution to the incessant thirst for more beyond what we really need for our wellbeing is merely a change in attitude. Major surgery is not required. Many cultures already assert that peace, serenity, and happiness are the answer, and are worth more than possessions. All we have to do is adopt part of their philosophical approach to life. We're not talking about becoming hippies, living in a commune and only eating organic vegetables, rather taking a different perspective on where we're going and what we're doing. Maybe the following story better illustrates what we mean.

A wealthy, successful, and very busy US businessman found that he increasingly enjoyed his vacation time in Jamaica. He flew there for two weeks every year and it always seemed to bring him so much peace and inner harmony. He relaxed for the only time in the year. He felt real and like himself. He felt good and healthy. He even found he slept well and didn't have to take any of his pills to relax and sleep. He always chartered a small boat and went fishing with the same old man who was a relaxed, happy, and friendly sort of chap. They would fish and generally pass the time chatting about sports and life. No high-level business-strategy discussions. No posturing or acting. They were just being themselves.

One summer, on arrival, the businessman found the old man sitting on the dock by his boat and told him excitedly that he had been thinking... He said that the immense pleasure and value he reaped from his Jamaica time could be monetized. He told the old man he had drawn up a spreadsheet and developed a business plan for him. He could send down a stream of friends, a guaranteed market, who would also love to rent the old man's boat. In fact, the businessman said, he would help the man raise capital in order to buy a few boats. Even a fleet of boats! He said he might also want to invest in a taxi and that way vertically integrate his business and make money on the transfers each time from the airport. He may want to think about getting into the accommodation and lodging business, too.

The businessman highlighted that the initial investment may be a bit stressful, but after a few years of growth, the old man would begin to amortize the cost of his fleet of boats and taxis, and after five years would be set. This business was a sure thing and he would be able to retire in a few years and not have to worry about a thing. He could then spend the rest of his life in his little old boat, taking it easy and going fishing every day with friends.

Progress is undoubted, yet the direction of some of our present attitudes remains worrisome. There is no guarantee that the positive trends of the past will continue into the future. Perhaps the United Nations Sustainable Development Goals (SDGs) offer a framework with which we can measure future progress, and guide our actions of the present. Designed to build on the Millenium Development Goals (MDGs), they are a set of 17 goals, including health and wellbeing, education, and sustainable cities, and which represent "a universal call to action to end poverty, protect the planet, and ensure that all people enjoy peace and prosperity".[5] Sustainable business expert Simon Pickard believes them to be a significant improvement on the MDGs for two reasons: while business had little engagement in the definition and delivery of the MDGs, the new goals are seen as valid criteria to shape long-term investment decisions material to core business. Furthermore, the statistical progress towards the MDGs (signed in the year 2000) was massively distorted by China's development, meaning that the global picture looked a lot rosier than the reality.

Whatever path we follow, the next 50 years will bring an unprecedented level of change that requires us to adjust our mindset for a fulfilling life.

Many cultures already assert that peace, serenity, and happiness are the answer, and are worth more than possessions.

THE SUSTAINABLE DEVELOPMENT GOALS

01   No poverty

02   Zero hunger

03   Good health and wellbeing

04   Quality education

05   Gender equality

06   Clean water and sanitation

07   Affordable and clean energy

08   Decent work and economic growth

09   Industry, innovation, and infrastructure

10   Reduced inequalities

11   Sustainable cities and communities

12   Responsible consumption and production

13   Climate action

14   Life below water

15   Life on land

16   Peace, justice, and strong institutions

17   Partnerships for the goals

Almost at the top

This is a personal story. The story of two Scotsmen who met in Barcelona, each having made the city their home after a similar path that included Scotland, the US, and Spain. The secret stairway we introduce at the beginning of this chapter links Steven's home in Sarrià to Rory's in Vallvidrera, and we aim to share a love of Barcelona through some of our own experiences, the city's rich history, and the showcasing of moments that have allowed our own wellbeing to soar as our careers have progressed. We aim to play our part in making Barcelona a world leader in workplace wellbeing, a place global talent is drawn to as people wish to leave their mark for a better world, and have fun doing it.

Steps have been central to human progress throughout history. The pyramids of Egypt, the ancient Incan city of Machu Picchu, and the Phoenician Steps in Capri have all allowed human beings to climb ever higher or connect with previously inaccessible parts of their world. The next time you walk the 40-odd steps across one of your rooms at home, imagine for a second where those 40 exponential steps would take you. Our aim in *Chief Wellbeing Officer* is to accompany you on those steps as a means of changing your mindset to the world around you.

Rather than reserving such a mindset for a technology-focused context, what is the moonshot you can aim for in your own life? We hope you enjoy the journey, and the steps you take through the chapters of this book. Our wish is that the impact these steps have on you, for both your personal and professional life, will result in your very own moon landing. Let's keep climbing.

2
THE
FOURTH
INDUSTRIAL
REVOLUTION

"I've seen things you people wouldn't believe. Attack ships on fire off the shoulder of Orion. I watched C-beams glitter in the dark near the Tannhäuser Gate. All those moments will be lost, in time, like tears in rain. Time to die."

Roy Batty, *Blade Runner*

BARCELONA was the first Spanish city to embrace the Industrial Revolution. With the natural advantages of a large port, the textile industry grew massively and raw materials were imported from around the world. The first railway line in the country was established in 1848, a year after the construction of the Liceu Theatre on Las Ramblas to cater for an increasing bourgeois class. The new-found wealth led to the 19th-century *Renaixença* (Renaissance), a heady time of artistic and economic growth that returned Barcelona to its medieval heights of great prosperity. However, the city became a victim of its own success and by the mid 1850s the city was on the brink of collapse. The population of 187,000 lived in a tiny area, confined by the city's medieval walls, with population density more than double that of Paris. Life expectancy was 36 years for the rich and just 23 years for the working classes.[1] The government eventually bowed to the inevitable pressure to tear down the walls, but the problem then became how to house the growing population in the area around the old city.

Step forward Ildefons Cerdà, an engineer and progressive urban planner who had a clear vision for the 'expansion' he called Eixample. Cerdà designed to maximize sunlight, natural lighting, and ventilation in homes, the need for greenery in people's everyday surroundings and the efficient movement of people, goods, energy, and information. He seized the problems of the old city as a creative opportunity to improve the wellbeing of the people of Barcelona.

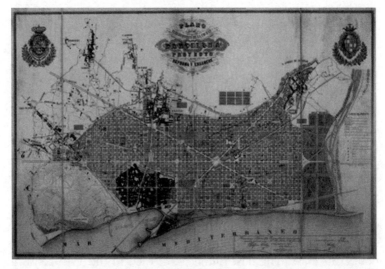

Figure 2.1. Original plans of the Eixample, 1859

We believe that the Fourth Industrial Revolution is also a creative opportunity. The human race stands at an inflection point in history, and our assessment of the present context and subsequent choices will determine whether we thrive or destroy society and order as we know it. It really is that serious. Never before has the role of Chief Wellbeing Officer been so crucial, not just for companies but also for humanity. We must all get involved.

From zero to four – how did we get here?

First we developed steam power to mechanize production. Throughout the 1700s, various iterations of steam power and piston machines developed, but it was not until James Watt (another Scot!) developed his engine that the technology became applicable and useful. Many scholars say that this invention paved the way for the British Empire. The Second Industrial Revolution came with electric power. Mass production became possible and the very nature of work was altered. Many more things could be made for more people, and these were far cheaper than before, thus the masses could participate in the benefits produced. That is, they could afford a Model T Ford – it was not just for the rich! Then came electronics and information technology, driven by microchips with memory capacity and processing power that was unthinkable before. Just like cars became available for the masses in the previous Industrial Revolution, computing was possible in every household. Finally, we get to where we are today: 4IR. It builds on the third but is, like the previous ones, a step change. Now we consider the digital revolution with all its connectivity and exponential technology. We see a fusion and overlapping of technologies (biology, physics, chemistry, engineering...) and even the fusion of man and technology.

The first three revolutions started with a key innovation and then lasted for decades, or even centuries. The fourth one is much faster. Never mind change, rapid change is the new normal. The speed of current breakthroughs has no real precedent,[2] with exponential growth taking over from the previous linear reality. The numbers are so astronomical they can be difficult to grasp.

The impact of these emerging technologies is at every level and so profound that every single human and non-human living organism may be impacted by it – not to mention at a societal, governmental, or company level. Another important aspect of the 4IR is that we are already committed. There is no going back. All we can do is steer it in a certain direction. It will affect the very essence of what it is to be human, with the creation of new machines perhaps making us even more human.

Let's step back for a second. Look up at the stars. There are, we think, 100 billion galaxies. One of them is ours, the Milky Way, which is made up of 100 billion suns. Our sun (that is, one of those 100 billion) is somehow positioned at just the right distance from a certain rock in order to make our existence possible, but not inevitable. The universe has evolved for about 15 billion years and it gave birth four billion years ago to our planet, Earth, with its atmosphere, its water, and its vast variety of living things.

The numbers are hard to fathom. Our minds are not built to handle such numbers. However, our minds themselves are as complex as the very universe around us. We may be discussing the emergence of superhuman machines, but each of us is already equipped with a machine of astronomical complexity. Like the universe with its 100 billion galaxies, the brain has 100 billion neurons and innumerable synapses, at least 1,000 times more than the number of neurons. That is over 125,000 trillion switches in a single human brain.

To put it simply, the universe is awesome, but so are we. Ultimately, 4IR is not about machines, it is about humans. People with values.

Like the universe with its 100 billion galaxies, the brain has 100 billion neurons and innumerable synapses, at least 1,000 times more than the number of neurons.

People with the power to shape their future. There will be an ability to connect these people, to count on their collective wisdom, to enhance their collective knowledge, but not necessarily at the cost of individualism and liberty. A collective moral consciousness could prevail to shape our destiny. Collective reasoning will be more valuable than before, leading to creativity previously unimagined. There is no better time for us as humans to consider both our own and collective wellbeing, with changes afoot to potentially maximize that wellbeing.

The first task will be to use new technology to rid ourselves of the hangovers from other revolutions, including our unthinkable quantity of waste, massive overuse of plastics, and dependence on fossil fuels. Then we can move towards potentially staggering rewards, such as heightened standards of living, enhanced safety and security, and the development of superhuman ability. Machines will supply us with the insight and perspective we need to reach those solutions. But they won't supply the judgment or ingenuity. People will.

The major medical breakthroughs of the previous industrial revolutions were about having a massive impact. There were mass vaccinations (the eradication of smallpox, for example) so epidemics were almost forgotten, and basic hygiene came to all. Countries needed people. The measure of a country's development, something we touch on in the next chapter, depends on its population, and everything was done to increase the total. Countries needed armies and the economy needed employees. Size mattered! In contrast, individualization will matter more than ever in the future. Today, small countries including Switzerland and Singapore top the rankings for competitiveness.[3] The 4IR will scale-up such efficiencies, with individualization developing within commerce and extending to education, medicine, and beyond.

For thousands of years everything was geared up to defend us from 'acts of God'. Famine was humankind's worst enemy. A small mistake in the sowing of the crops, or error of judgment in choosing the right field, a run of bad harvests and millions of people would starve. In fact, as recently as 80 years ago, millions of people died from famine in Europe. Less than 20 years ago four million died from famine in the Congo. Epidemics killed millions well into the 20th century, with Spanish flu taking 100 million lives less than 100 years ago. That's more than the combined impact of both world wars.

According to Yuval Noah Harari, in his epic book, *Homo Deus: A Brief History of Tomorrow:*

> "In ancient agricultural societies human violence caused about 15% of all deaths, during the twentieth century violence only caused about 5% of deaths, and in the early 20th century it is responsible for only 1% of global mortality. In 2012 about 56 million people died throughout the world; 620,000 of them died due to human violence (war killed 120,000 people, and crime killed another 500,000). In contrast, 800,000 committed suicide, and 1.5 million died of diabetes. Sugar is now more dangerous than gunpowder."

Though there is an undoubted worldwide pandemic of type 2 diabetes, it is still only the ninth leading cause of death, as we see in figure 2.2 below, with heart disease and cancer the main causes. In any case, Harari's point is that war, with no remaining justification, is not a likely event. Previously, the main source of wealth was assets like gold and diamonds, and countries went to war to get them. Now, in 4IR, the main source of wealth is knowledge. You can attack and acquire an oilfield through war but you cannot acquire knowledge that way. He adds that we now have new problems. We may have, for the most part, solved famine, plague, and war but more people now die from eating too much than eating too little. More people commit suicide than are killed by soldiers, terrorists, and criminals combined. The average human is more likely to die from eating a Big Mac than from Ebola or drought.

LEADING CAUSES OF DEATH IN PERSPECTIVE

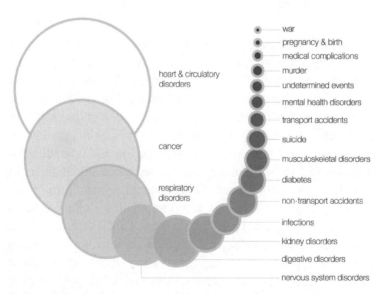

Figure 2.2. Leading causes of death in the UK, adapted from the NHS Atlas of Risk

The end of death?

In the past, death was unconquerable. Now, in 4IR, it is seen as merely a technical problem that will be solved. Humans can now act with the superhuman powers we used to give deities. Greek, Roman, and Hindu gods were especially good at giving life, as well as causing war, pestilence, and famine. They were literally superhuman, but most things that made them 'above' human can now be accomplished with drugs or biotechnical engineering. And the current exponential growth in machine intelligence will make us even more godlike. The connectivity and convergence of augmented reality, cloud computing, nanotechnology, big data, and 3D printing, to name but a few, will push the boundaries on what is human and what is machine. Indeed, humans will increasingly have both organic and non-organic enhancements. After a while, we may not even be able to determine how much is human as digital, physical, and biological features are enhanced. But we will be better!

Perhaps the most compelling efforts we are seeing are the current life-extension projects, carried out not by governments, but the current technology titans. Companies like Google, through its project Calico, have invested more than a billion dollars focused on using the tools of technology – that is the chips, software programs, algorithms, and big data they use in creating an information revolution – to better understand and upgrade what they consider to be the most complicated piece of machinery in existence: the human body. Other examples include the work of Larry Ellison, who has donated half a billion dollars towards anti-ageing research. Then there's Peter Thiel's Breakout Labs that exist to fund radical science and bold ideas, including projects to grow bones from stem cells, research ways to repair the cellular damage that occurs with age, and ways to quickly cool organs in order to preserve them. Sergey Brin of Google, who has a gene associated with Parkinson's, has given $150 million to efforts that use big data to understand DNA. He thinks these could rapidly transform research into Parkinson's (and other diseases), providing the keys to avoiding neurodegenerative diseases that cut life short. Not wanting to be left out, Mark Zuckerburg is awarding million-dollar prizes to support scientists whose discoveries extend life.

This may seem a little futuristic, but it is a current fact that for every year of life, life expectancy increases by three months. Most of us will live significantly longer than our parents, and many babies born today are expected to live for at least 100 years. Women born in South Korea in 2030 are projected to be the first in the world to have an average life expectancy above 90,[4] a far cry from 1850s Barcelona. And these projections do not take into account the potential changes from the technology advances outlined above. The implications are that across the space of the next two generations, individuals, institutions, and governments will have to accommodate two, possibly three more decades of life.

There are significant social and philosophical consequences to this extended life. A large part of our drive, belief systems, and creativity comes from the inevitability of death. George Bernard Shaw said it was death that gives us purpose in life:

> "I want to be thoroughly used up when I die, for the harder I work the more I live. I rejoice in life for its own sake. Life is no 'brief candle' for me. It is a sort of splendid torch which I have got hold of for the moment, and I want to make it burn as brightly as possible before handing it on to future generations."

Steve Jobs shared a similar sentiment in his 2005 Stanford commencement address, urging people to find their true self in the limited time we have available. Reflecting on his own initial near-death experience he viewed death as "very likely the single best invention of life. It is life's change agent."

Will you be happy gardening all day?

The great opportunity, assuming we can focus on personal and mutual wellbeing instead of destruction, will be the pursuit of happiness. To be specific, the new project of the 21st century and 4IR is gaining immortality and bliss. The Greek philosopher Epicurus (341-270 BC) taught that the purpose of human life was the pursuit of happiness, which could be achieved by the measured study of the natural world and adherence to a prudent and temperate hedonism. He added that the blind pursuit of more money (more aligned with the Third Industrial Revolution) will only make us miserable. Epicurus added that "being happy does not come easy!"

Yet as we touched on in the opening chapter, happiness hasn't increased with the recent technology advances that will continue to characterize further movement into 4IR. Advanced technology-based societies such as South Korea have a suicide rate 30 times that of developing countries including Peru, Guatemala, and Ecuador.

Another consideration of 4IR will be the effect on employment. If we consider that many of today's jobs will disappear through automation (9-90% of today's jobs by 2050, depending on the study), what will happen to one's purpose, and related happiness, that is a result of daily work? Of course, new jobs will appear as has been the case with previous technology disruptions that have been examples of job destruction, such as bank ATMs. These machines actually freed up bank workers to focus on more value-added services for their clients, resulting in a rapid increase, not decrease, in bank branches.[5] Nevertheless, not everyone will be able to retrain, and governments are today looking at the effects of mass automation and the feasibility of introducing a Universal Basic Income for all citizens. The concept of gardening leave may take on a whole new meaning for a transitionary generation.

Under the current global education model, kids who have a high IQ and study well at school choose a particular field when they are about 18 years old and get a place at university. They are there for three or four years and then work in a company for the rest of their life. The rest of their life is the next 40 years or so. They don't learn much in those years but they work hard, and at the age of 60 they retire and live off their pension. This picture will be quite different if people are living to 150. It won't just be about learning and then working in two big chunks. It will be a constant interchange of work and learning. People will have much longer careers and will have to reinvent themselves constantly. We may soon be working until we are 100 and lifelong learning will be the key! We look closer at this personal reinvention and disruption in chapter seven.

In any case, it is clear that many more of us will need to look for meaning beyond our daily struggles. There will certainly be more space in our lives, and people must realize this will be an opportunity. A new education model will help the next generation deal with the new normal.

A is for algorithm

Education will undergo extreme change. Students will not be trained to be merely job-ready – the focus will be on becoming future-ready. Being adept at thinking rather than knowledgeable in a specific subject will be of greater value. How can we teach people to do jobs that don't yet exist? More specifically, there will be far more time provided for connection as well as for deep reflection. Everything will be done to nurture creativity and entrepreneurship. Education so far has been geared specifically for an industrial economy. In fact, not much has changed since the days of Plato: we sit in rows, listen to the oracle speak, and don't ask questions. We teach students to follow instructions and manage facts. But this, after all, is what machines are good at. Let us leave the computers to do what they do well, and we can get on with loftier pursuits.

Happiness, for example! Humans are better at thinking out of the box. Thus we must set students free. This will not merely be the era of freedom of speech but rather, freedom of thought.

Humans are good at connectivity and we should nurture this in school and university. Deep connection is essential for wellbeing, and we should encourage it at an early age. The new technologies available to us are a tool and we should use them responsibly. Even gaming is about making connections – indeed several authors, including Yuval Noah Harari, who we have noted here, and Mihaly Csikszentmihalyi, who we cover in the next chapter, have commented that the more life and work resembles a game, the more rewarding it is, and the happier we are. Storytelling, our ancestral means of communication, also increases connection. It is what differentiated us humans from the larger-brained Neanderthals, and delivered us victory over them. We must develop, learn, and improve this innate ability. Education needs to foster connections between humans and enhance collective wisdom. It needs to identify what kids are good at, and while assuring their basic skills are good enough, needs to help kids improve those strengths. In this way we will be fostering not mediocrity, but individual excellence.

We are beginning to see the seeds of a new education model. Students now have more opportunities to learn at different times and in different places. E-learning tools facilitate opportunities for remote learning and at the pace desired by the individual. Classrooms are increasingly being 'flipped', meaning that the theoretical part normally taught laboriously in class is learned outside the classroom, using different online means, and the practical part and what was previously homework is taught interactively in the classroom with other students, through discussion and debate. Learning is becoming far more tailored to the specific needs of each student, with the 'oracle' teacher becoming more of a facilitator and coach. Project-based learning (with several schools in Barcelona leading the way worldwide) is increasingly being used at an early age in

place of developing subject expertise in order to dri
orative problem-solving and teamwork that will ch
future of work.

The near future of learning will include much more personaliza-
tion, just like medicine. Students will learn with study tools that
adapt to their own capabilities. 'Gifted' kids will be challenged with
more demanding materials, and those with learning difficulties, or
below-average ability may be offered more time and opportunity
to practice until they can raise their level. Teachers will be able to
see who needs help, or who needs to be challenged more. There
will also be more in the way of choice, and students will be able
to modify their own learning process. Digital machine tools will
also be employed to act as personal tutors, in whatever field is
necessary. Skills currently taught in business schools, such as
collaboration, time management, and even entrepreneurship, will
be taught from a much earlier age. The pedagogical methodology
will develop multiple intelligences, not just IQ and the regurgi-
tation of facts. Exams will change completely, with coursework
and class participation being celebrated more than relying upon
day-long written exams as a way of measuring a student's acumen.
There will also be more in the way of field experience, with students
completing internships, mentorships, and even apprenticeships
at an earlier age than we see today.

Education will of course continue for life, supporting the personal-
reinvention dynamic that we note above. The organization may
provide the physical environment and stimulus for this learning
process but the onus will be increasingly on individuals to invest
in themselves. The democratization of learning – as evidenced by
the world's leading universities, including Harvard and Stanford,
making their content freely available online through Massive
Open Online Courses (MOOCs) – shows that the future will be led
by curious, driven individuals, not just those who studied hard for
a few years when they were a teenager.

For continuous learning, executive education, and personal disruption, Singularity University in Palo Alto could represent a model for a future 4IR world. Launched through a collaboration of science and industry, including Amazon and Google, its campus is located at the NASA Ames Research Center. The 1960s hangars, weird machines from the Cold War, and general Space Race feeling give a taste of the past and urgency around the future – you feel as though there's about to be a mission launch. University content is driven by identifying global challenges and bringing together a diverse talent pool to address them – this may include actors, screenwriters, entrepreneurs, savants, and even astronauts in addition to scientists and academics. Adding students to the mix, usually from companies, the university creates a type of open-source collective wisdom to "prepare you to seize exponential opportunities. Our mission is to educate, inspire, and empower leaders to apply exponential technologies to address humanity's grand challenges." The curriculum changes so fast that accreditation for the courses isn't possible, with emerging technologies in artificial intelligence, nanotechnology, and digital biology, creating an inspiring environment. Our own experience there, though expensive at around $200,000 for a week-long team workshop, creates a convincing vision that the future will be one of abundance and opportunity for all.

The Fourth Industrial Revolution sounds like a solely technological concept, but it will be the biggest step for liberty, freedom, and equality that humankind has ever made. With responsible actions, supercomputers, big-data processing skills, human physical enhancement, cyborgs, and the leveraging of collective wisdom will unite to create a new free abundance for all. True happiness will be the goal and never before has the role of a Chief Wellbeing Officer been so important. Through education we can leverage the radar of technology and hone the compass that is humanity.

Merging the best bits of humanity and technology will create many more visionaries who can look beyond the walls of our present reality. Ildefons Cerdà was one such visionary of the First

Industrial Revolution. He invented urbanization, with his work on the expansion of Barcelona representing the first meticulous scientific study on the use and possibilities of a city as a place fit for human habitation. He was able to see into a bright new future. The chamfered corners of the new city blocks was his idea to deal with traffic, allowing people to see more clearly what was happening left and right. Cars had yet to be invented, but when he discovered railways he figured there would soon be "some sort of small machine powered by steam that people could park in front of their houses".

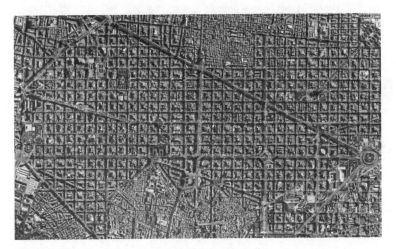

Figure 2.3. Aerial view of the Eixample today

Though not all of his vision for the Eixample was realized due to political squabbling, a lack of trust from architects, and the greed of speculators, who, for example, rejected his idea for gardens in the middle of resident blocks in favour of more residences, this grid pattern with octagonal intersections remains a significant influence on the present day in which Barcelona is playing its part in 4IR. Recognized as a global leader in areas such as smart cities, mobile technology, and the Internet of Things, such technological advancement and progress will only be sustained, we believe, if the city nurtures the wellbeing of its current residents, and attracts the best global talent available who are prepared to make Barcelona their home.

3

RESTORING HUMANITY TO LEADERSHIP

"I'm sorry Dave, I am afraid I can't do that."

HAL 9000, *2001: A Space Odyssey*

IT WAS the hot Barcelona summer of 1926. A man had been hit by a tram and lay dying on the road. Nobody cared much because he looked like a tramp. But appearances can be deceiving. This dishevelled individual made one of the greatest contributions to the city, with his work becoming famous around the world. And he wasn't alone in making a significant contribution to Barcelona's wellbeing. Something was certainly in the air in the 20th century, as Salvador Dali (1904-1989), Joan Miro (1893-1983), Pablo Picasso (1881-1973) and Pau Casals (1876-1973) all made their mark. All lived long and full lives, surviving into their nineties. All were driven by a well-defined purpose in life, were marked by idiosyncratic and unique behaviours, and all had an unthinkable, unimaginable, often incomprehensible vision of what sort of world they wanted to inhabit.

You may ask what we have in common with such great creative figures. Well let us explain. It revolves around the simple things we can all do to bring humanity back to leadership. We believe an egotistical form of leadership has taken hold in recent years and many have forgotten the simple fact that leadership is about others.

In our leadership development work we focus on certain elements that indeed concern the self, managing and leading the self better,

51

but which have the ultimate goal of being directed towards others. Whatever way you take and apply Chief Wellbeing Officer, we believe you will practice leadership. Leading others to be the best version of themselves, purpose, vision, and values are all an integral part of the rationale of wellbeing at work, and the best organizations allow for these elements to be present, regardless of a person's role or seniority.

Purpose

Professor Hugh Simpson, Rory's father, spent four years on a scientific base in the Antarctic in the 1950s. At 21 years old he was the base doctor to the 15 men serving the Falkland Islands Dependency Survey. They lived in a tiny hut and only had contact with the outside world twice a year when a Royal Navy Ship would check in and leave supplies in the summer. For nine months each year they were alone on a windswept shore, at the foot of a mighty glacier, on a deserted continent.

Years later, at home in the Scottish highlands, Hugh would sit around the fireplace with his family and recount his Antarctic adventures. It became clear that the experience had marked his life. Even though the subsequent 60 years were to fill with academic and scientific accomplishments, as well as adventure and endeavour all over the world, his four years as a young doctor in a frozen hut on that frozen continent had left its impression. They were days of strife and true survival. There were long cold nights and storms that sometimes lasted for months. The small group of men would huddle in their hut and ride out weeks and months of whiteout and blizzard. When the weather improved they would go off on expeditions to map the interior and conduct scientific experiments and research. Sledging trips with husky dogs. They would chart new territories, literally making maps and claiming land for their country. They would even leave their names on the maps for all of posterity. In all, Hugh sledged an incredible 6,500km with his dogs, in areas where no man had gone before.

They observed incredible, magical things: whales being trapped by the ice in the bay and frantically thrashing their way towards escape; millions of penguins marching past; seal colony wars; husky dogs inadvertently charging off an ice cliff and taking everybody with them; and a man in a boat being swept out to sea by strong katabatic winds, never to return to base. They even discovered a cave that had been inhabited by shipwrecked US sailors from the great whaling days of the 19th century.

They all felt a strong sense of purpose in what they were doing. They were there for their country, to further science and protect the continent, and Hugh to medically care for the team. The vast majority of his patients were actually the husky dogs, which always seemed to fight and tear each other's eyes out. He would sew them up, try not to be bitten, then send them out again into the cold.

He did have one human patient, though. One man went mad. He could not stand the concept of isolation and was the only person on the base that did not have a specific task other than to help out. He was the so-called 'gash hand'. He was not a medic, a mechanic, a botanist, or a geologist. He was just there to generally lend a hand in whatever task. As far as he was concerned he just had to pass the time and make some money. He had no interest in Antarctica itself. He attacked another team member with a carving knife, giving Hugh a serious problem: they only had relief twice a year and it was midwinter – they were not going to see anybody for eight months, yet they had a lunatic living with them who at any time could try to kill somebody, or himself. The only alternative was to medicate the man to keep him groggy, and watch over him in his bunk until the ship came eight months later.

Hugh believed the man went mad because he had no real purpose. No daily interest. No real task. Nothing to get his mind around. No affiliation with the mission. On the long nights of conversation and debate, the man had nothing to talk about. All he could do was reminisce about home: green England. The lack of purpose and belief in their mission or cause was the reason he fell apart. To be clear, it was not because his role was less sophisticated than the others, it was due to the fact that he had no interest or desire to be there, except for the money.

Even the animals there had a purpose and they clearly felt it. The huskies were essential for transportation and adventure. Hugh would lead small teams on month-long sledging trips to map the land. The dogs always slept outside, always fought, were always hungry but they were happy and proud. The happiest dogs on the planet, Hugh would say. They knew their role and sensed their importance, and the men loved them. They had a purpose and they knew it.

However humble the task, it's up to you to make a choice: do you believe in what you are doing? What is your contribution? Are you doing the best you can do?

A story from Rory

I haven't been in the army or the Antarctic, but I did work at Disneyland. I cleaned tables and emptied trashcans, flipped burgers, and manned the cash tills. It was all very menial, but in all those tasks I had a belief and pride in what I was doing. Disney had not been part of my upbringing or my family culture, but when I first saw the kids smile when they spotted Mickey Mouse in person I realized I was part of something worthwhile. I didn't care about the Disney global enterprise and its pursuit of market dominance in the three segments of media, theme parks, and merchandising. All that was irrelevant to me – corporate bullshit – but what I did know was that I was helping make children happy.

For the first time in my life I reflected on the different attitudes of my fellow workers (or 'cast members' as they call them at Disney). Some worked minutes into their break in order to finish a simple cleaning task. Others stopped the second their shift was done and would leave a table half cleaned. They preferred to have three minutes more of break time than have any personal fulfilment in what they were doing. Who was happier? Who enjoyed life more? Who had pride and believed in what they did? It was so clear to me which group felt more accomplished, which was happier and which one I wanted to be in. It was a simple choice.

What amazes us when we teach company executives is when we ask them in class: "What is your purpose?" and they reply, "What purpose? Oh yeah, I'm here to hit my KPIs, my targets, to do a better job for the company, make the company more money and make me more money." The more philosophical ones may say: "I'm here to provide for my kids." That's great, we say, but purpose is not a person or people, it is bigger than that. Purpose is consciousness. Purpose is what separates us from being algorithms or animals. Pop philosophers say that soon humans will be replaced by machines that have better algorithms than we do, thereby relegating us to 'animal status'. That may be true, but only if we haven't found our purpose. What we need to do is define our purpose, share it, be proud of it, and use it to clearly define what to focus on.

After all, everything has a purpose. Look around where you are right now. Take it all in. Every single thing you see has an easily definable purpose. From our homes we can see the great city of Barcelona: the port has the purpose of harbouring ships, the elegant W hotel on the beach accommodates rich tourists, the Sagrada Familia cathedral (so says its modern-day architect) has the purpose of providing awe, wonder, and religious comfort. If you are sitting down, the chair's purpose is to support you, the carpet to improve the feng shui of the room. So if all you see around you has an easily explainable purpose, then how is it that when we ask the executive students in our classes, who may be just like you, about their purpose they look at us with stupefaction? This is baffling. Mind-boggling. Everything we see around us has a purpose, yet we haven't taken the time to reflect on what ours is? Purpose is all-powerful and gives us direction in life. Moving towards it delivers us happiness, even if we are penniless.

Simon Sinek insists on the importance of purpose in his now famous TED Talk of September 2009 in Washington.[1] He talks of an individual's purpose, but also that of the team and company. He says people don't buy what you do, they buy *why* you do it. He reminds us of the Wright brothers and their purpose to achieve powered human flight. They competed with Samuel Pierpont Langley, who had all the budget, knowledge, and advice from the greatest consultants of the day, but no real purpose, other than a desire for fame. We all know that the Wright brothers did it, taking off on 17 December 1903, and the aircraft industry was born. Purpose got them through countless setbacks, accidents, and economic challenges. They had a constant belief that they could do it. A dream. And they did it.

What we need to do is define our purpose, share it, be proud of it, and use is to clearly define what to focus on.

TO LOCATE, DEFINE, AND CLARIFY YOUR PURPOSE, A GOOD START IS TO REFLECT ON THE FOLLOWING QUESTIONS

Consider the week you have had. Remember the moments of each day, the actions and tasks, no matter how small. When one of these memories makes you smile, you have stepped on something that is close to your purpose.

Now look back over your entire life. Remember the high points, moments of joy and/or accomplishment. Recall your greatest successes or victories and really try to reconnect with how you felt.

What special talents or skills got you there?

What makes you cry with emotion?

What are you really passionate about?

What do people most admire about you?

What have you always wanted to do but never done? What do you dream about doing? What would you do if weren't afraid?

What do you know that you can give to this world? What is your unique speciality?

Values

If purpose gives us direction then values inform us how to act. Our values are the operating manual in terms of how to get things done. There's a multitude of ways to do things, but what is your way? Which action and behaviour aligns with the authentic you? Which way will make you feel guilty, and which way will make you feel proud? Dictators, tyrants, and CEOs like to quote Machiavelli in that "the end justifies the means". But a basic class in ethics tells us it should be the other way round – that is, "the means shall justify the end". If you go down a path of actions that are not aligned to your own code of conduct, your ethic, then in the short-term you may achieve some goal, but the long-term result will eventually feel shameful. You might get to the top of the metaphorical mountain you were trying to climb, and quickly, but if you killed your support team in doing so, the victory will not just be bitter, it will be completely unfulfilling, not to mention scuppering your journey back!

So what are your values? Which ones do you choose? Once elected or identified they will help align your actions with your purpose (your direction) in life.

In class we ask people to shout out examples of values, words that describe their ethical code. They usually start a little shy. Nobody says anything until somebody states in a hesitant voice "quality", then somebody else shouts "customer care", and "service". At this point we step in and make it clear that we are not talking about corporate values. We don't care about those nice words written on the wall that accompany the company mission. What we need to identify are the individual's values, and hope that the corporate values align with these, not the other way round. If they don't align then in order to be happy the employee should probably leave the company, or strive to alter the so-called corporate values. So we start again and ask for examples of values. Somebody shouts out, "justice!", then somebody else says "freedom", then "loyalty", and then the cascade of words flows from the group. Passion, compassion, solidarity, peace, fairness, justice (again!), truth, tenacity, determination, generosity, charity, coherence, consistency... and so it goes on. A nervous voice will inevitably say "love" and the audience proclamations will eventually begin to peter out.

Research shows we could probably continue the exercise up to about 100 values. Apparently there are around 100 words, at least in the Judaeo-Christian world, that could be referred to as values. No doubt if we added all the other religions there would be a large overlap and maybe many more. The point is that if we look at our past behaviour we will notice common themes. We should expect the usual suspects regarding how we act when the chips are down. In those moments when we had to take a stand there will be a value, or two, that always seems to appear. The key is to identify it and own it as yours. You may also get to know what your key values are by reflecting on the times that you didn't take a certain course of action and in hindsight felt guilty or ashamed of yourself. That feeling of guilt is valuable in itself. That awful gnawing sense of shame is screaming at you to help define yourself and determine how you will act on future occasions.

Our values are indicated by our behaviour. In fact, values inspire our behaviour. Our values tell us how to act given a particular context. A good way to identify and pinpoint these values is to reflect on your favourite possession or purchase. This behaviour, this feeling of pride, reward, and comfort will give you an idea of what is important to you. It is an indication of what is of value to you. This may be something very materialistic, and that's OK, we are merely trying to understand what gives you a warm feeling and makes you feel happy. That thing may be a technological device like your slick-looking and highly functional MacBook, the rock you bought in a fossil shop on your honeymoon, a framed family photograph, the Chanel bag that gives you so much confidence, your new Specialized road bike, a Thermomix, Church's leather shoes, Rolex, or even the bright Asics running shoes that just make you want to put them on and run and run and run.

Whatever it is, however big or small, expensive or cheap, try to identify the few material things that make you feel good. We are not saying you would die for these things, or that you would rescue them from a burning house before your dog or grandmother, we are just suggesting that the warm feeling these things give you can help indicate something important about you. This doesn't mean you are driven by possessions or by impressions or by having more than your peers. No, it's just that we all value some things more than others, and this is a very personal thing that says a great deal about our persona.

These things and our behaviour around them can indicate important aspects of who we are. We cherish some things that others find trifling. Yet there are other things we do not value that others hold sacrosanct. That's OK. Nobody is being judged! The key is to realize what these things are and try to understand what they say about you.

Our values are indicated by our behaviour. In fact, values inspire our behaviour. Our values tell us how to act given a particular context.

Consider the following questions:

Think of those high points of elation, success, and joy. What was special in what you did or how you performed?

Now consider the darker moments, when you failed or were deeply troubled or sad about something. How did you behave? If it was a failure caused by your actions, or if you 'misbehaved', what old weaknesses or negative patterns are most closely associated with that failure?

What are the negative/destructive trends in your behaviour that causes pain to others or yourself?

What makes you angry?

What behaviour of others really drives you mad with rage? Which traps do you tend to fall into?

What are you most afraid of?

Who are your heroes? What do they stand for and which qualities do they possess?

Recall a time in your life when you made a stand on an important issue. When you stood up for something, or somebody, even at personal risk. What values were you protecting at that time?

Recall a time in your life when you did not intervene or protect somebody and something, and afterwards felt deeply ashamed about it. (That guilt is good, because it can help you identify the values you truly cherish but have not had the confidence to uphold.)

What is your favourite book or movie?

What would you be prepared to die for? If it's an idea, person, or possession, ask yourself what value(s) they represent.

Vision

If purpose was the 'why', and values the 'how', then vision is the 'what'. Purpose gives us orientation and direction. Values help us align our actions accordingly, and vision is the desired destination.

The vision has to be crystal clear. As Seneca the Younger said: "If one does not know to which port one is sailing, no wind is favourable."[2] This means that unless you actually have a clear image of where you want to be and what the best 'you' looks like, it is unlikely you will achieve it.

There is no limit as to how bold the vision may be, but the key is that it is realistic given where you are now. If you are obese and you imagine yourself looking like an athlete, that's OK, but be cognizant of how far you need to go.

Vice Admiral James Bond Stockdale had something to say about the importance of vision, but also reality. On 9 September 1965, while flying on a mission over North Vietnam, Stockdale was hit by enemy fire. He ejected and parachuted into a small village, where he was severely beaten and taken prisoner. He was then held as a prisoner of war in the infamous Hanoi Hilton for nearly eight years, where he was routinely tortured.

He was already a hero, but he didn't stop at that. He slit his scalp with a razor to purposely disfigure himself so his captors could not use him as a propaganda tool. They covered his disfigured head with a hat, so he then beat himself with a stool until his face was swollen beyond recognition. He also slit his wrists in an effort to prevent his captors torturing him into revealing sensitive information. Stockdale was hardcore!

Many years later, in the business book *Good to Great*, Jim Collins writes about a conversation he had with Stockdale regarding his coping strategy during his time in the Vietnamese POW camp: "I never lost faith in the end of the story, I never doubted not only that

I would get out, but also that I would prevail in the end and turn the experience into the defining event of my life."

When Collins asked who didn't make it out of Vietnam, Stockdale indicated it was the ones who were unrealistic about their situation. "The ones who said, 'We're going to be out by Christmas.' And Christmas would come, and Christmas would go. Then they'd say, 'We're going to be out by Easter.' And Easter would come, and Easter would go. And then Thanksgiving, and then it would be Christmas again. And they died of a broken heart." Stockdale added: "This is a very important lesson. You must never confuse faith that you will prevail in the end, with the discipline to confront the most brutal facts of your current reality, whatever they might be." Collins described this as the Stockdale Paradox: the appreciation of one's brutal reality, but with an all-powerful positive vision. That vision was supported by appreciating what he did have: a life, a wife, a passion, a great life journey so far, and that he would have that again one day.

Visualization in sport is well appreciated. The 100m runner has to see herself cutting the winning tape, the marathon runner has to imagine himself entering the Olympic stadium, the crowd going wild, as he completes his last few laps of the track and wins gold. He must imagine himself on the podium, bending for the medal and feeling the weight of gold around his neck. He must visualize these things months, years, even decades in advance. If he cannot or does not, then it is not going to happen.

As a young child growing up far from London in Dunblane, Scotland, Andy Murray imagined himself winning Wimbledon. That image of victory stayed with him throughout all his years of training, through the losses, the many near misses, and also the years spent in Barcelona, away from his family, at the famous Sánchez-Casal Academy. He changed his coach and worked on his head game to burnish supreme tennis ability, winning Wimbledon for the first time in 2013. The feeling he had when he lifted the famous trophy was not alien to him because he had "seen it" and "felt it" for years.

In the study of sports biomechanics there is research that shows that merely imagining an athletic action actually improves the muscle responses and brain synapses in order to perform that sport. This is the true power of visualization.

The idea that we can actually change reality just by thinking is known as the Pygmalion effect. The name originally comes from Ovid's narrative, in which Pygmalion was a Cypriot sculptor who carved a woman out of ivory. He fell in love with her and lost interest in real women. Later, Aphrodite gives the ivory girl life, and as Pygmalion kisses the statue he feels warmth and the statue loses its hardness, becoming human.

The hard data comes from a famous experiment often referred to as The Harvard Rats. The research is frequently embellished, used out of context, and hotly debated. A Harvard psychologist, Bob Rosenthal, told his research assistants he had identified two types of rats. One group were super-rats. Gifted rats. He explained that through a process of selective breeding he had genetically created the Arnold Schwarzenegger of rats. Strong, intelligent, and creative. He called them 'maze-bright' rats. He also had a group of dumb rats referred to as 'maze-dull' rats, and suggested that these had basically been chemically lobotomized. The poor things could hardly stand.

So the researchers proceeded with their typical maze experiments. They timed the rats as they ran through the maze and went for their cheesy reward. The research assistants were actually having fun: competition always made their research work more entertaining. The super-rats were given names and treated like celebrities, like the way a prize-fighter might be revered, or a wonder cock from the fighting rings of the Philippines. They would caress them, and some even started taking bets on which rat would get through the maze the quickest.

Figure 3.1. Super-rat

Then there were the dumb rats, poor things. They were off loaded on to their racetrack without much of a thought, and the researchers actually felt pity for them. The results came in and, as you may have guessed, the super-rats were the best. They were the elite athletes. The dumb rats were the slowest. The poor performers. They got to the cheese eventually, but generally their track times were lamentable.

Only once all the results were collated, Rosenthal explained they all came from the same control group. No selective breeding had been done. They were all the same! The rats performed according to the way they were 'seen' and the way they were treated. Those that were seen as super-athletes, envisioned as winning and gobbling up the cheese, were the ones that did. This is the Pygmalion effect, and the power of positive vision. A vision of what you want the future to look like. The dumb rats never had a chance as nobody even thought they were capable. It was the perfect example of a self-fulfilling prophecy.

"When we expect certain behaviours of others, we are likely to act in ways that make the expected behaviour more likely to occur."

Bob Rosenthal, 1985

Rosenthal then turned the experiment on to kids.[3] He worked with Lenore Jacobson at an elementary school in San Francisco in 1963. They told teachers that they had identified bloomers. Bright kids. Kids with more talent and ability than others. They told the teachers who the bloomers were and followed their results. As predicted by the rat experiment, the students who were labelled as gifted, despite being chosen at random, ended up with higher grades and developed into more successful students. Rosenthal called this the expectancy or Pygmalion effect. Again, the bloomers had been picked at random. They had no special qualities. The above-average academic progress was the effect of favourable teacher expectations. The teachers would encourage them more. The teachers would 'see' them graduating top of the class and going on to do great things – even becoming president of the United States! The Pygmalion effect had encouraged the kids to do better.

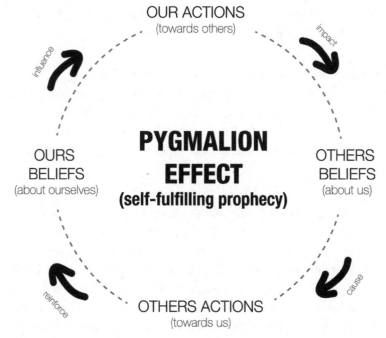

Figure 3.2. The Pygmalion effect

Vision is not just how you see yourself and others, it is also how you see the world around you. Einstein said that the most important decision you will make in your life is whether or not you live in a friendly universe or a hostile universe. It is your choice. Yes, a choice. Happiness is not an automatic state that is achieved when crossing the appropriate wealth line. When you choose to live in a hostile word, all you find and hear is bad news: you wake up in the morning and your back hurts, the coffee is bitter, your damned car is uncomfortable, the damned traffic is a menace, people don't know how to drive these days, and you want to kill your boss. The opposite is true as well. When you choose to live in a friendly universe; you start to see opportunities everywhere and hear more good news. You find good people. It doesn't mean there is no more bad news, it's just that you decide not to focus on it. Mood is contagious, especially important to remember if you lead others. Make note of the effect you have on your team and the people around you if you come into work with a grumpy face.

Leadership is not a mystical thing that is hard to grasp. It is not an intangible essence that has to be assimilated through some kind of transcendental quest. Rather, it is a real thing that can be mastered by all. By reflecting closely on purpose, values, and vision, a more human-based leadership will take you to the moon and back.

Now let's go back to that man dying in the street: Antoni Gaudí died at the age of 74. Half of Barcelona dressed in black to pay homage to their popular hero, the creator of many of the city's most famous buildings, parks, street lamps and benches. Gaudi was driven by a strong purpose, which was to celebrate the work of God by creating architectural forms derived from God's work: nature. He used his engineering, design, and architectural mastery to synthesize neo-Gothic, Art Nouveau, and Eastern elements to create structures never imagined before. He said, "nothing is art if it does not come from nature" and "originality is returning to the origin". He had a vision, not just of mighty structures, but also of whole cities and modern living industrial ecosystems that were part of nature. Gaudi was buried in a crypt of the edifice where he had worked for the last 43 years of his life, the Sagrada Familia. To this day its mighty, avant-garde, weird, incredible, futuristic, awesome, crazy, structure continues to rise into the sky and will keep gaining height until its completion scheduled for the year 2026, 100 years after Gaudi's death.

4

THE **ROI** OF WELLBEING

"We should strive to welcome change and challenges, because they are what help us grow. Without them we grow weak like the Eloi in comfort and security. We need to constantly be challenging ourselves in order to strengthen our character and increase our intelligence."

H. G. Wells, *The Time Machine*

THERE ARE many dates in Barcelona's history that, given their significance, have a clear sense of a before and after. The construction of the Eixample in chapter two is one, and the political tensions around 1 October 2017 another. 17 October 1986 is surely one of the most important. This was the date that Barcelona was selected to host the 1992 Olympics that utterly transformed the city and its people. As well as the usual construction of sports and hotel facilities, major infrastructure projects were initiated that significantly impact the wellbeing of residents still to this day. The Olympic Village was constructed at the port, opening the city to the sea, making it fit once again for leisure, and transforming the coastline from an industrial area to what *National Geographic* now calls the best beach city in the world. Other major projects included modernisation of the airport with two new terminals, and construction of the city ring roads to reduce traffic congestion in the centre. Does it matter that the Games had one of the highest cost over-runs in Olympic history? In an age where the Olympics is under increasing scrutiny regarding sustainability and legacy, Barcelona is held up as a success case rather than one of the most debt-laden in history. What is the return on investment (ROI) of any significant endeavour? Should it be measured only in monetary terms?

Measuring progress and performance

Societal wellbeing is increasingly recognized as being of vital importance for progress worldwide. It is widely accepted that measurement of economic growth in itself isn't a true reflection of moving in the right direction, and governments are looking closer at ways in which they can measure development beyond gross domestic product (GDP). Though GDP is a standard and long-standing measure of development it is viewed by many as flawed. Gross national product, the forerunner to GDP, was the subject of criticism in 1968 by US President John F. Kennedy:

> "Our gross national product... counts air pollution and cigarette advertising and ambulances to clear our highways of carnage. It counts special locks for

our doors and the jails for the people who break them. It counts the destruction of the redwood and the loss of our natural wonder in chaotic sprawl... Yet the gross national product does not allow for the health of our children, the quality of their education, or the joy of their play."

Though garnering little interest at the time, his remarks have since become well-known, as governments, including France in 2007 and the UK in 2010, have commissioned studies into new measures of national development and progress. Such recent focus builds on other alternative measures to GDP, such as the human development index – developed by the United Nations Development Programme and first published in 1990 – which combines income, life expectancy, and education. Much of this work led to the sustainable development goals that drive progress today and which we discussed in chapter one.

So which areas are governments looking at and how are we doing? Since 2011 the Office for National Statistics of the UK Government has used a mix of 41 subjective and objective measures of wellbeing, including life satisfaction, health, income, relationships, and crime. In 2017[1] it found areas that are improving include job satisfaction, education, personal finances, community belonging, and satisfaction with leisure time. Areas that are deteriorating include levels of anxiety, mental wellbeing in general, quality of relationships, and regular participation in sport.

The Scottish Government has made societal wellbeing a core part of its stewardship of the country. The National Performance Framework is, according to Cabinet Secretary John Swinney, about "how people live their lives, how they want to live their lives, their aspirations, and their hopes in society". The 61 indicators comprising the framework are a measure of societal wellbeing and are driven by the five strategic objectives of: Wealthier and Fairer, Smarter, Healthier, Safer and Stronger, and Greener. Great

Scottish thinkers from history inspire this new vision, including Adam Smith,[2] who said:

> "No society can surely be flourishing and happy, of which the far greater part of the members are poor and miserable. What can be added to the happiness of a man who is in health, out of debt, and has a clear conscience?"

Wellbeing is therefore well established today as an important part of a thriving society. Business, as a key part of society, therefore has a role to play in this wellbeing and many organizations are considering other measures, beyond shareholder value, to gauge their development and progress. Recognizing that non-financial measures of progress still support economic growth helps to mainstream this more holistic approach, with research, for example, showing that higher job satisfaction leads to an increase in firm value.

What measures should be used to gauge wellbeing at work? And what use does this wellbeing have for the business? Researchers at the Ross School of Business have looked at the factors that support sustainable high performance.[3] They focus on the term 'thriving' to describe employees who are not just satisfied and productive but also engaged in creating the future. They see thriving as present when people believe what they are doing makes a difference and that they are learning. Thriving employees are highly energized and know how to avoid burnout. They found people who fit their description of thriving as having 16% better overall performance (as reported by their managers) and 125% less burnout (self-reported) than their peers. They were 32% more committed to the organization and 46% more satisfied with their jobs. They also missed much less work and reported significantly fewer doctor visits, which meant healthcare savings and less lost time for the company. Professor Scott DeRue, dean of the school, is convinced of the increasing importance of wellbeing for leadership and performance. He highlights the concept of 'spillovers', noting that wellbeing isn't just something that matters at work: "We've found that if people aren't well at work, they aren't well at home, and vice versa." The impact of business on healthy communities and societies is clear, with encouraging signs being a change in attitude with the new generation of managers. Current students at Ross have a thriving Wellness Club which tackles some of the main issues around health and performance that DeRue sees as important for more positive organizational leadership.

In 1776 the philosopher Jeremy Bentham defined the fundamental axiom of his work to be "the greatest happiness of the greatest number that is the measure of right and wrong". Bentham's premise was a key element leading to today's fascination with happiness and engagement in the workplace. He valued the importance of friendship in developing wisdom, saying "friendship dances around the world, bidding us all to awaken to the recognition of happiness". He meant that it was friendship and connection that ultimately delivered happiness. As we covered in the last chapter, the Fourth Industrial Revolution will help us connect like never before. It is up to us to make the most of that.

The 2017 World Happiness Report includes a chapter on Happiness at Work. Loosely defined as subjective wellbeing, the authors consider self-reported evaluations of happiness in different jobs and around the world. Labour intensive jobs are rated as having lower levels of happiness worldwide. In contrast, white collar jobs – executives, managers, officials – evaluate the quality of their lives as higher. Self-employment has a more nuanced effect, in being

We've found that if people aren't well at work, they aren't well at home, and vice versa.

associated with both higher overall life evaluation and with more negative, daily emotions such as stress and worry. It is important to highlight the key part that work in general has on our wellbeing as human beings – unemployment is shown to have a devastating effect, with the authors commenting that:

> "The importance of having a job extends far beyond the salary attached to it. A large stream of research has shown that the non-monetary aspects of employment are also key drivers of people's wellbeing. Social status, social relations, daily structure, and goals all exert a strong influence on people's happiness."

A key finding for our pursuit of business impact through wellbeing is the fact that though relatively high levels of happiness and job satisfaction are present around the world, engagement at work is still low. The authors state that engagement is a higher hurdle to clear than the simpler concept of satisfaction. How may we therefore gain that higher state of performance as opposed to idling along? An answer may come from a classic approach to wellbeing that has enjoyed a resurgence in recent years. The work on 'flow' by Mihály Csíkszentmihályi[4] has been covered of late in terms of performance, yet it is important to remember that its roots are in the pursuit of human happiness and wellbeing. What this tells us, we believe, is that wellbeing and performance are inseparable – and offer an as-yet-untapped source of massive potential for a company. At the very least both concepts are interdependent given the right workplace conditions. If we can better cater for the wellbeing needs of the company leadership and workforce at large through optimal experience and engagement, as proposed through flow, significant value may be generated on all sides.

Often associated with artists and athletes, who are understood to do their best work when they're 'in the zone', flow has been found by researchers around the world in different activities. Reflecting on designing autotelic jobs – those that provide conditions for people to be highly engaged, regardless of external rewards such as money or power, Csikszentmihalyi believes that work should resemble a game. The feedback element as shown in the quote that follows may be a part of one's leadership activity. Providing feedback is a powerful motivating factor that aligns with people's purpose and shows them that what they are doing really does matter.

The further challenge for managers is to design work that stretches people to use their skills. When the work itself requires skills outside the capability of the worker, anxiety is the result. When the worker is tasked with a job that doesn't require their full set of skills, they become bored. Moving in and out of the flow zone would be expected, given the dynamic of the workplace, and so effective people management should include being aware when excessive anxiety or boredom takes hold. A continual advance to the upper right of the graph is the overall aim. If we take the need for continual workplace learning as a requirement for well-being, as stated in some of the research above, then applying these developing skills to the challenges of the workplace should result in the organization exhibiting continual advancement also.

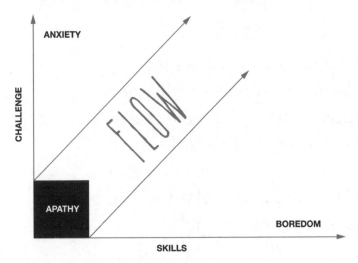

Figure 4.1. The flow channel[5]

"The more a job inherently resembles a game – with variety, appropriate and flexible challenges, clear goals, and immediate feedback – the more enjoyable it will be, regardless of the worker's level of development."

Mihály Csíkszentmihályi

The business approach to wellbeing

Wellbeing, happiness, satisfaction, engagement, experience, performance – all are impacted significantly by work. How may we best capture the available value? Wellbeing has a formal presence in most large companies today, yet it exists at a relatively junior level of the organization and is focused on the reduction of risks, including absenteeism and sickness. Many programmes take a clinical-based approach rooted in the insurance industry. Absence is often reduced, yet the dangers of *presenteeism*; long hours and low productivity, or people returning to work before they are ready, and affecting other members of the workforce negatively through sickness or emotions, are increasingly recognized.

Are formal wellbeing programmes required? In most cases, yes. Yet there is another way of perceiving the opportunities of wellbeing, in the ways that it can improve executive performance – through the increased energy, creativity, resilience, and leadership it undoubtedly generates. If a more progressive definition of health exists beyond merely the absence of sickness, why does health and wellbeing management in the enterprise still suffer from a similarly negative approach? One answer could be that the narrow, risk-focused view of wellbeing at work is easier to measure. Some of the business leaders we have engaged with believe this to be part of the company journey – gaining the foothold of demonstrating impact on such measures before affecting the leadership culture.

Elsa Belugou has managed wellbeing at O2 in the UK for several years. She counts on board-level sponsorship helping immensely in gaining 'airtime' for a topic that can be difficult to maintain, especially in times of turbulence and transition – certainly true in the telecommunications sector. She feels businesses need to have wellbeing as part of their DNA and that this should be driven from the top down. She has also started asking people who have suffered from mental health issues to write a personal blog to ensure it becomes normal at the company to talk and ask about these issues, further promoting a healthy discussion culture. Key measures for her own ROI include engagement, absence (or lack of!), utilisation of services, and interaction at company events.

BeHealthy is the health and wellbeing brand at Banco Santander. Global head of HR, Roberto di Bernardini has an ambition to eventually track the financial impact of the programme, but takes a five-year view instead of the short-term, believing instead in the value of gaining visibility and participation around the world. He is convinced of the business benefits of health and wellbeing, highlighting the massive difference in managing people compared to 30 years ago. There is now, he believes, a greater consensus around the importance of taking a holistic approach and taking care of people, both professionally and personally: "It's not just about their professional or skills development but making them better human beings, and this necessarily involves physical and mental health. We have a duty to look after our humans while the science also shows that this personal development has significant professional benefits." Interestingly, much of the leadership development and performance management links to this development. Now 40% of the company's approach to performance management looks at how they are perceived as a leader – through their daily behaviours – by their direct reports, peers, and superiors.

Our own experience goes beyond the narrow confines of a risk-focused wellbeing programme towards leadership development, which in turn affects organizational culture. The discrete behaviours of leaders influence the behaviours of the people they lead – indirectly through the example they show or directly through their people management – allowing a wellbeing culture to emerge that mirrors the thriving environment noted by the Ross School of Business. This also aligns with some of the recent work in organizational culture by PricewaterhouseCoopers, which advises that tackling the 'critical few behaviours' is a more feasible approach than trying to change culture directly.

The business impact of wellbeing

The financial benefits of wellbeing programmes is a matter of debate. The Rand Corporation found that although four-fifths of all US employers with more than 1,000 employees are estimated to offer such programmes, there are no cost-savings associated with the management of high-risk employees (those who smoke or are overweight). It contrasts its findings[6] with Johnson & Johnson, one of the longest-running programmes in the US, which finds return on investment ranges from $1.88 to $3.92 saved for every dollar spent, believing its own methodology to be more accurate. It also found participation in programmes to be low, in the range of 20-40% of the workforce.

In the *Wellness Syndrome*[7] the authors concluded that corporate wellness programmes not only provide low returns on investment but can actually backfire, making many employees less healthy and more anxious about their jobs. One reason is that they are aggressively marketed and often alienate those high-risk people they are trying to help out in the first place, such as people who are smokers or overweight. Attaining the publicized image of the 'superfit' employee is often so unlikely that people don't bother trying, while the recent trend towards measurement through wearable devices forms part of the big-brother mentality that can alienate workers.

So the benefits of wellbeing at work are undoubted, yet wellbeing programmes don't always capture that value. How then may we deliver the ROI of wellbeing? One area could be talent management. Attracting, developing, and retaining the best talent is a priority for many leading companies in today's business environment. Today's war on talent and the sometimes-flighty nature of the millennial generation means that companies need to look at any conceivable edge to maintain and nurture their most precious resource. Wellbeing has a potentially massive part to play. Santander's Di Bernardini states that:

> "We are no longer competing against Citi or Lloyds but also Facebook, Google, and the fintech start-up in someone's backyard. We need to convince people that working with us, while of course involves making money, there is a responsible and sustainable purpose at the core of everything we do."

As the case below demonstrates, established companies who used to count on their own brand lustre to ensure loyalty and engagement can no longer do so. The emerging liquid workforce will only increase such phenomena. Accenture predicts that 45% of the workforce will be based on a contractor model by the year 2025, and have three or four main employers.

A case from Professor MacGregor

It was the second morning of the annual graduate onboarding event when the chief human resources officer of one of the biggest technology companies in the world got the call. She sat wide-eyed as she was informed that 50 of the 300-strong group wanted to go home. The onboarding experience hadn't met their expectations apparently. So she flew in a day earlier than planned to meet with her new, mutinous charges. They thrashed out a deal. The group of 50 had to design a new onboarding experience that would not only satisfy them, but also receive the buy-in of the other 250. "You better get a move on" she said, before leaving. "I'll be back this time tomorrow."

The gig economy throws up a number of different dilemmas. Whose responsibility is wellbeing? The marketplace for talent will compete on the basis of the wellbeing offering they make available, including broad aspects like purpose. Today, people look beyond the pay packet to the wider conditions and the possibility of leaving a positive mark.

Current rapid development in people analytics ought to support the business case. Ralf Buechsenschuss, global manager in Nestlé's People Analytics function, uses these rich data sets to inform better decision-making in the business. People management is one of the main areas of focus. It includes measuring the impact of diversity and the benefits of better people management skills in line managers – essentially measuring the positive business impact of leadership. The team works as a type of in-house consultancy, where data scientists are tasked with different projects based around a key question, such as the impact of training on business results or levels of customer satisfaction. He sees even greater potential of using data responsibility to look at organizational health and performance of people in the business. In general, he views the growing capability in people analytics as a means of differentiating the company in today's marketplace for talent, while also giving the chief human resources officer the data to back up decisions and engage in more strategic-level discussions with the CFO and CEO in a company, referred to in some quarters as 'the golden triangle'.

Getting to the critical few behaviours of wellbeing at work

What elements need to be considered for a culture that supports the Chief Wellbeing Officer? Much of our own work has centred on physical activity, sleep, mindfulness, and nutrition. Much of this development has taken place at Telefónica's corporate university, Universitas, which we believe to be the best in the world. In many ways Universitas is about wellbeing rather than strategy, and content is designed according to the ROI of being rigorous, original, and impactful. The four areas of physical activity, sleep, mindfulness, and nutrition are introduced briefly below as a first reflection on business impact. We then detail the content in part two of the book, which follows.

Physical activity has been shown to support different business outcomes. Meetings are a large feature of business and changing the dynamic of meetings, from sitting to standing or even walking, can have a variety of positive business impacts. The business case is supported by our human biology. Movement creates energy in the oxygen-rich blood that is transported through the body and brain, activating neurons and releasing hormones conducive to better cognitive performance. The behaviours we demonstrate as leaders should show the right example for the rest of the organization. Simple things like getting away from your desk for more direct communication, and the accidental encounters that drive innovation may help create a thriving organizational culture based on wellbeing. Though spending time on dedicated physical exercise is often viewed as a luxury, it helps create the energy required for a demanding job, reduce stress, and improve self-efficacy that can be transferred to other areas of life.

Sleep has a key role in high performance, especially for the most senior people in an organization. Executive thinking, as we noted in chapter one, requires us to be flexible, agile, and innovative, responding to a changing environment. It is the type of thinking that suffers most with sleep deprivation – even a slight reduction on what you need as an individual (with most of us needing between seven and eight hours).

Mindfulness has enjoyed significant attention in business over recent years. Brain-imaging techniques show that it actually does change the brain. Human development specialist Christina Congleton and her colleagues, writing in the Harvard Business Review blog[8] highlight two of the eight affected areas of the brain most pertinent to the business context. The anterior cingulate cortex (ACC) is associated with self-regulation, meaning the ability to direct attention and behaviour, suppressing inappropriate knee-jerk responses, and learning from past experiences. Meditators have been shown to have more activity in the ACC. The second area is the hippocampus, which is covered in receptors for the stress hormone cortisol. Studies have shown that this can be damaged by chronic stress, and the practice of mindfulness has shown development in this area, therefore supporting resilience.

Mindfulness is a very specific and valuable technique that addresses the dangers of busyness. Though excessive multitasking and a lack of focus aren't exclusive to the current generation of mangers, such characteristics are certainly more prevalent in recent years as a result of technology. The distracted world in which we live was the focus of Cal Newport's book, *Deep Work,* which shows how quality thinking, and the success that ensues, can be achieved in spite of the current environment. The modern take complements timeless wisdom such as Peter Drucker writing in *The Effective Executive* in 1966 that "if there is any one secret to effectiveness, it is concentration. Effective executives do first things first and they do one thing at a time."

Nutrition has been shown to affect decision-making. Well-cited research by Professor Shai Danziger and colleagues[9] into the decision-making processes of a jury panel in Israel found that the chances of getting parole were 90% lower in the afternoon. They highlight the 'decision fatigue' of judges having to rule all day on cases without sufficient breaks. An important part of the subsequent redesign of the process was paying attention to the food intake of the judges, in order to sufficiently fuel their decisions. Decision fatigue can be traced to Roy Baumeister and colleagues, and their research on willpower as a muscle. They consider the energy requirements of the brain, which, like many muscles in the body, requires glucose to function. We have long believed that the best decision-makers are the ones who know when *not* to trust themselves, and part of that distrust can be related to nutrition. We have considered measures of food such as the glycemic index (GI), which can result in fluctuations of glucose in the body and corresponding energy fluctuations. Habitual consumption of high GI foods, of particular danger for the busy professional while travelling, can have negative effects on decisions as well as weight management.

It follows that physical activity, sleep, mindfulness, and nutrition should all be considered for wellbeing at work, not just for the benefits of health and wellbeing, but to support the business case and performance of the people who work there. With this clear business case in view, wellbeing should therefore be present beyond a narrow wellbeing programme, to leadership development in the enterprise. Such programmes, though potentially valuable in certain circumstances, will have a limited return on investment. Leadership development, focusing on a critical few behaviours based on wellbeing and performance, will create the necessary conditions for flow and a more balanced, positive, and thriving organizational culture.

There are signs of this happening. We have worked with many pioneering companies in this regard, through the coaching and customized training programmes for senior staff, yet it is far from being a normal part of leadership activity and the overall culture of work. Chief Wellbeing Officers are therefore required in all organizations, and at all levels of the organization, regardless of formal job title and responsibilities.

In a similar fashion to moving beyond the flawed measure of GDP to gauge national development and progress, we need to move beyond the flawed view that wellbeing only regards the absence of sickness and reduction of absenteeism. Instead, what is the positive business impact that can be achieved through wellbeing? This necessarily includes elements of engagement and experience. The next part of the book will begin to unpack the main components of wellbeing at work, which we view as healthy, happy and high-performing.

Our fervent wish is that wellbeing is used as the means to build value, not to fix something that is broken or patched on after other things have been sacrificed. We have often encountered people who have espoused a strong message of responsibility – perhaps CSR in business or environmental care. You then find out that their reinvention came after five years as an investment banker or some similarly ethically questionable industry. Come on! We applaud any attempt at reinvention but find it a bit rich coming from people who only turn to this direction once they have €5m in the bank. Let's try and celebrate another way to success and merely tolerate this, not the other way round.

The 1992 Olympics put Barcelona on the world stage, where it has stayed ever since. The ROI of the massive infrastructure spend may be questionable if viewed only on narrow terms. It becomes more convincing when viewing how the city has become a truly global pull for tourism. Yet the biggest benefit may be in the deep cultural change of the Catalan people. The Olympics gave them confidence and belief, changing their daily behaviours forever to truly embrace wellbeing.

PART 2

WELLBEING

The second part of
Chief Wellbeing Officer unpacks
the WHAT of our vision, detailing
the main content blocks of holistic
intelligence and the rhythms of our
lives on which wellbeing exists

5

LEADING THROUGH EMOTIONAL INTELLIGENCE

"The heart is not like a box that gets filled up; it expands in size the more you love. I'm different from you. This doesn't make me love you any less. It actually makes me love you more."

Samantha, *Her*

NESTLED at the bottom of our secret staircase from chapter one is Col·legi Montserrat. The number-one ranked school in the whole of Spain, it caters for children of all ages, from pre-school to university entrance. There are several features that make Montserrat unique and of increasing prominence worldwide. An innovator in using project-based learning (PBL) teaching methodologies for many years, it leverages the latest findings in neuroscience to develop multiple intelligence, believing in the importance of physical, intellectual, spiritual, and social excellence. Founded in 1926, it is run by missionary nuns, the Daughters of the Holy Family of Nazareth.

This is the first chapter in part two of *Chief Wellbeing Officer*: 'Wellbeing' will uncover the content base, or WHAT of our vision. We begin by presenting a wider view of intelligence. 'Total' intelligence has guided our work for over a decade and is the core concept from which we believe a more thriving workplace can emerge. We present this over the next two chapters. Here, we introduce the concept of the holistic leader and focus on the leader as a human being through the development of emotional intelligence or EQ. In the following chapter, we consider the leader as an athlete, and develop the often-neglected concept of physical intelligence or PQ.

The holistic leader

Ever since the European Enlightenment of the 17th century, philosophers, sociologists, and scientists have debated how to measure intelligence. Paul Broca (1824-1880) and Sir Francis Galton (1822-1911), a cousin of Darwin, were among the first scientists to actually come up with a scaled measurement; a quantifiable measure of intellect and mental capability. They thought they could determine intelligence by measuring the size of the human skull. They assumed that the larger the skull, the smarter the person. Their studies later took a sinister diversion and turned into fully-fledged eugenics (meaning 'well-born'). This early version of genetic engineering was later used by certain governments to eliminate genetic traits they thought could lead to low intelligence, poverty, or a 'contamination of the Nazi master race'. In any case, it seems absurd today that physical features such as skull size could be used to determine intelligence or capability. However, the methodology used for intelligence quotient (IQ) tests used by most higher education authorities and companies today is perhaps just as inexact and arcane.

The IQ test was developed in 1904 by Alfred Binet (1857-1911) and later adapted by Theodore Simon (1873-1961). Yet it was never intended to measure intelligence but rather ignorance. The French Ministry of Education asked these researchers to develop a test that would distinguish mentally disabled children from 'normal' ones. New laws had been passed in France that required all children to attend school, and the government wished to identify which children would need special assistance. Binet realized that some children were able to answer more advanced questions that only older children were generally able to answer. Based on this observation, Binet suggested the concept of a mental age, or a measure of intelligence based on the average abilities of children of a certain age group. This first intelligence test, referred to today as the Binet-Simon Scale, became the basis for the intelligence tests still in use today. However, even Binet himself did not believe that his psychometric instruments should be used to adequately distinguish intelligence levels in normal children. Binet stressed the limitations of the test, suggesting that intelligence is far too broad a concept to quantify with a single number. Instead, he insisted that intelligence is influenced by a variety of different factors.

However, the fuse had already been lit, and over the years there was increasing demand to measure, scale, and rate intelligence of not just children, but university entrants, as well as company and army recruits. IQ tests were even used to screen immigrants arriving at Ellis Island, New York, to see if they would make good citizens of the United States. Generalizations were unfortunately made that encouraged the US Congress to enact immigration restrictions on huge swathes of people who were unfairly judged as being unfit to enter based on 'low intelligence'.

For more than 150 years, school-teaching methodologies have grown up around the IQ measure. The focus of almost all of our school teaching and school texts has been to drive data into our kids and then measure how well they can regurgitate it.

Beyond our schools, companies also have overstated the importance of IQ. When it comes to hiring new employees, IQ trumps everything else. Despite what looks like a sophisticated recruitment process with awareness tests, psychometrics, and extensive essays and interviews, companies generally hire new employees based on their IQ and not much else. If the candidate sounds intelligent and has good exam results then they tend to get hired. All this despite the knowledge that IQ does not correlate with success, leadership ability, or even strategy formulation. IQ does not get you to the top of the company. IQ does not indicate your ability to innovate, motivate, or lead, It merely tells you that you are not mentally deficient.

Furthermore, recent studies point to the fact that the more senior you become in your company, the less important IQ actually is. An excessively high IQ may actually be a disadvantage for a CEO. It can encourage focus on numbers and processes rather than people. After all, such focus is often the reason for promotion in the first place. Unfortunately, 'what got you here won't get you there'. One may have excelled at school, then university and then in a company because of hard computational skills, mental agility, and an impressive ability to remember facts. However, it is clear that over time what becomes more important are leadership-based people skills. Soft skills, if you like.

So there's more to it than IQ. Effective leaders need to develop more of a holistic range of skills and abilities. A broad range of experience and know-how that, of course, includes IQ (for example, a knowledge of the business, processes, and data), but also softer things regarding how you interact and empathize with people, how you motivate yourselves and others, and how you inspire others and get the most out of them. Passion ensures that you are the best version of yourself and that you encourage others to do the same. Your creativity and authenticity are key. We call this broad knowledge base 'total intelligence'. It incorporates

IQ (traditional intelligence), EQ (emotional intelligence), PQ (physical intelligence), and SQ (spiritual intelligence). IQ is represented by the head, the heart stands for EQ, the body PQ, and the soul SQ. The important thing is to have equal development of all four. A balance.

IQ is of course important. This includes an understanding of the business and sector that you are in. It is having a grasp of the strategy of your company, its strategic options, as well as an awareness of what other companies are doing. It is having a knowledge of the processes and systems that operate around you. This is data, finance, operations, and business intelligence. It is business acumen.

Spiritual Intelligence, or SQ may be a deeply personal thing, yet it offers much potential in a team setting. Not necessarily religious, SQ may be viewed as the purpose, values, and vision that we developed in chapter three. In our many years' experience in business schools and universities around the world, as both student and professor, there has never been any time given to the importance of purpose. As for values, we often lay out corporate culture but it is usually wishful thinking, and the behaviours of the company are usually a long way from the stated corporate values. And though all companies talk about their vision, it is usually a corporate platitude lacking authentic language. SQ is not difficult. After all, it is all about you. Your personality and your authenticity. In the Stanford commencement address we noted in chapter two, Steve Jobs also said that: "Life is short, so don't waste it living someone else's life."

Reflecting on the questions in chapter three will help you develop your SQ. The following questionnaire is a quick way to get an idea of how you are doing in all dimensions. We follow with a focus on EQ.

TOTAL INTELLIGENCE: QUICK QUIZ

IQ

01 Have you started a book in the last month?

02 Do you spend more than one hour a week playing games: Sudoku, crossword, backgammon, or chess? (Digital games are included.)

03 Have you started a MOOC or online learning course?

04 Have you ever watched and shared a TED talk?

EQ

01 Do you sometimes get your team together socially away from work?

02 Do you know the names of the cleaners and receptionists in the office?

03 Do you have a third place? (A venue/club where you get together with people outside your usual network/circle, where you are not judged by your professional or social status. This could be a chess club, a sports club, volunteering, or charity work.)

04 In the last month, have you delegated something you love doing? (Only answer yes if you have a specific example.)

PQ

01 Do you measure any health-related parameters? (Sleep, calories, steps, heart rate…)

02 Do you participate in intensive aerobic exercise where your breathing becomes forced?

03 Do you regularly sleep between seven and eight hours?

04 Do you pay attention to the nutritional content of what you eat?

SQ

01 Do you spend more than two hours a week meditating or reflecting?

02 Do you disconnect from technology once during the day for at least one hour?

03 Do you have a sense of purpose? Does your team?

04 Do you truly see failure as an opportunity?

Award one point for every YES answer. If you scored 16 you're probably lying to yourself! 10-15 you are doing well. Below 10 and you have some work to do. Balance is very important. If you scored 12 but were deficient in one particular area, work is also required.

Leading through EQ

Emotional intelligence has only really been taken seriously since the 1980s, and many academics still say there are no hard measures that point to the correlation between high EQ and corporate success. In our opinion you only have to look at successful as well as happy people in your company to see that EQ is essential to get to the top. High EQ can be broken down into three main elements: communication, motivation, and empathy.

Communication

Communication is simple. All you have to do is make sure you are maintaining conversations with your boss, team, family, and yourself. Tragically, we seem to be losing this art. There are too many distractions from our smartphones, too much to do, and not enough time to actually bother with mere conversations. Ask yourself: when was the last time that you truly had a great, powerful, and profound conversation with your spouse, or your kids, or your boss?

Conversations are a priority if you truly want to lead. They should come first and be carried out authentically. All too often, especially at work, we use words that are not our own. In a desire to be politically correct, as if human resources is listening to every word, we fall short of having real conversations. In addition, we often use corporate mumbo jumbo and platitudes that make us sound like the annual general company report. We talk mealy mouthed about leveraging our assets, satisfying customer needs, maximizing value, up-skilling, reskilling, downsizing, and restructuring... Worse, we sometimes get home and keep spewing out the psychobabble. Be you and use your own language! Be authentic. You are better at being you than anybody else.

A key part of a conversation is listening. Listening for at least half the time. There's listening and then there's *real* listening. Listening to listen. Listen to understand. As Stephen Covey said, "Seek first to understand." Listening in order to add something to what is being said, not to add your point irrespective of what you are hearing. The chart below summarizes the six levels of listening.

6 LEVELS OF LISTENING

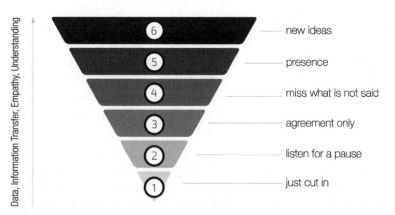

Figure 5.1. Six levels of listening. Own adaptation of the five levels of listening by Stephen R. Covey

At level one we are just rude. No sustainable leadership is going to result from level one listening. There may be times when, as a leader, we have to dip down to level one, but only very occasionally. Level two is not much better, except that you are a little less rude. The person you are talking to stops for a breath and you jump right in and go on regardless of anything said so far. At level three you are still not doing so well because you are missing so much. Level four is good, but there's a lot written between the lines, a lot of signs, signals, body language, and meaning that you are failing to pick up on. Level five is excellent. You are fully present. Level six is nirvana. You are gleaning all that is around you and are perfectly aware. You have entered a special place with the person you are talking to, where new ideas abound.

It won't always be possible to stay at level six, but as long as you can keep above level three, you will consistently be creating and making all around you feel affinity with what is going on. This is leadership. This is wellbeing as an individual and as a team.

Motivation

Motivation starts with you. If you are not passionate about what you are doing, you will fool no one. As a leader, your mood is contagious. So if you get to work and decide to enjoy the luxury of feeling a little down, a little flat, or anything other than exceptionally passionate for what you do, with a desire to bring the best out in yourself and those around you, then you will not be 'leading' that day.

Motivation may be about pushing people to face mighty challenges and bringing out the best in them, but it can backfire if you are encouraging people to do things you know they will fail at. If the goal is too great and the temptation is to let them fail anyway, then the person needs to understand that it was a long shot from the beginning. Let them fail gently. Failure, as we discuss in part three of the book, is a potentially valuable leadership tactic, but it has to be managed with care.

Motivation is about honesty. Outlining the challenges ahead, underlining the strengths needed to get past the challenges, believing that all the hurdles can be overcome, but being candid with what will be required. Motivation is about highlighting the contribution a person or a team will have if they do the right thing. It is about love, passion, and compassion. It is not about fear. It is not about what a person will lose if they do the wrong thing. Fear may motivate once or twice but it is not sustainable. Motivation with fear is not part of the wellbeing formula. It does not lead to growth. It does not add or contribute to anything in the long-run.

A great story (though hard to verify and discounted by several experts) which exemplifies pure, almost naive, raw motivation, comes from the famous Shackleton[1] advertisement placed in *The Times of London* on 29 December 1913. He was looking to build a team of diverse men who would have to live in close confines for years, and be the first to cross the Antarctic continent.

> ### Men wanted for hazardous journey. Low wages, bitter cold, long hours of complete darkness. Safe return doubtful. Honour and recognition in event of success.

The ad is short, honest, to the point, and yet extremely poignant. The emotion delivered to the reader leaves them thinking, "I want to be part of that noble endeavour". This frank and honest approach attracted 5,000 applications, which Shackleton sorted into three categories (a short list) labelled "mad", "hopeless" and "possible". Shackleton eventually selected his 27-strong crew from the candidates who went on to deliver one of the greatest feats of Antarctic exploration. Paradoxically, they failed. Their ship, *Endurance*, was crushed in the ice and mere survival became their primary objective. They had to leave the ship entombed in the pack ice and set off across the ice floes, dragging their lifeboats and launching the boats and rowing when possible. Eventually, after a great feat of survival, of trial and tribulations as ice floes split in two and threatened to separate them, of blizzards, whiteouts, freezing men, and hurricane-level winds, they reached the small Antarctic island, Elephant Island. This was the first time in almost 500 days they had stood on terra firma. They had travelled almost 500km and at first were happy to make camp on a rocky, wet, grim, tiny windswept beach, wedged between the Arctic Ocean and a mighty glacier that covered the island.

When it became clear that no help was coming, Shackleton and a few of his men set off again on what has become known as perhaps the most intrepid, crazy feat of nautical and navigational brilliance – in a quest for South Georgia, where they had passed through at the beginning of their expedition. They knew there was a whaling community and ships that could come to the rescue. 1,000km later, sailing the high, ferocious and freezing seas of the South Atlantic they arrived. Yet it still was not over! A storm caused them to land on the wrong side of South Georgia and they had to cross the mountainous island to reach salvation. This time it was a mountaineering feat of survival. They were unequipped to ice climb, cross crevasses, and wade through deep snow, not to mention they did not have a map. It took half a century for anybody to repeat the mountain adventure and only then with the latest climbing gear. On 20 May 1916, a year and a half since setting off from there, they walked into the whaling town. Shackleton and his two men were, in their own words, "a terrible trio of scarecrows, dark with exposure, wind, frostbite, and accumulated blubber". The hardy whalers were deeply affected by what they saw. It was unbelievable. Shackleton and his team had been written off as dead. Missing in action. Yet here they were walking along the beach. In any case, it took almost three months to eventually pick up the rest of the team on Elephant Island, but the incredible thing is that in the whole adventure, not one man had died.

When Shackleton and his men returned to the UK in 1917 the First World War was raging. Many men ended up as soldiers and a few died in the war effort. They had ironically swapped dying in the frozen Arctic seas for being gassed to death in the trenches. For many years Shackleton's exploits were forgotten, or written off as a failure. It wasn't for another 50 years that he was associated with endeavour and survival. It has been said more recently that

Scott can be lauded for the scientific method, Amundsen for speed and efficiency, but "when disaster strikes and all hope is gone, get down on your knees and pray for Shackleton".

Shackleton was all about raw motivation. His team failed in the probable but succeeded in the unimaginable. He motivated them to volunteer for the perilous adventure in the first place, he motivated them to leave their ship in the ice, he motivated them to work together despite much personal animosity, he motivated them to set off ill-equipped into ice and ocean and over mountains, and he motivated them to stay alive when all hope was gone. He was the epitome of a team leader. He got the best out of everybody, and it was his motivational skills that were most important. Essential. He made an incredible effort not to let the predicament drag him down; not to let on that he knew disaster and death for all was almost inevitable. He self regulated to avoid losing his cool when the men squabbled or yet another calamity befell them. He built trust through his actions, his generosity, his positive attitude and optimism, and he knew trust could be lost immediately if he flew off the handle and broke down.

A story from Rory

Are you motivated to die? Would you risk death on a daily basis for money? Probably not, yet through history there have been countless examples of those that do. The world's oldest and most dangerous profession is probably mining. Palaeolithic man mined haematite in Swaziland 43,000 years ago, searching for the pigment red ochre. More recently, about 7,000 years ago, we started looking for gold. Since then, mining has consistently been one of the planet's most dangerous professions. We have always died in droves underground, yet people still go there and they still die there. Is it merely money that encourages miners to spend 12 hours (sometimes 24 hours) a day, kilometers below the surface of the Earth?

While industry experts say the number of fatalities has decreased considerably since the early 20th century, there has been no shortage of tragic mining accidents in recent years. Most recently, as the last of the 33 Chilean miners emerged from the rescue capsule, there was jubilation around the world. The 2010 Copiapó cave-in incident was over. But the disaster that gripped audiences globally also serves as a reminder of the dangers of working in a mine. Although there are no accurate figures, estimates suggest that such accidents kill about 12,000 people a year.

At Potosí in Bolivia they have been doing it the same way ever since the Conquistadors arrived in 1492. I went down a mine, a kilometre underground with some kids. We slipped through some moist holes in the ground, crawled deep down and watched the kids with their tiny hands reach in and gingerly place dynamite in the fissures. We then scuttled and slid out of the way as the earthshattering explosions revealed fresh treasure, or not. The kids then rushed back, coughing through the smoke and choking on the dust, only to be disappointed and have to start all over again. This is archaic but it's not that different in the modern, state-of-the-art Ontario mines where I also found myself underground. There, they have heavy machinery but it is just as dangerous. So why do they do it? What motivates them?

The motivation varies, but there is a sense of pride in the air at all of these sites. It is seen as an epic endeavour to work underground. A noble pursuit in order to harvest the crops that Mother Earth *(or 'Pachamama'* in Bolivia) has delivered to us. Motivation comes from affiliation and a sense of purpose greater than economic reward. They love it! They really do, and those that haven't been down a mine cannot fathom it. Tradition also usually comes into the picture. Mining is a way of life and always has been for these people. There is often local clamour when, for some reason, the mines are closed – even though the authorities believe they are doing their people a favour.

Motivation comes when people feel there is a purpose, they feel affiliation and that they are part of the project: that they can make a difference. Motivation can be found even when the task in hand is repetitive and boring. If individuals feel they are contributing to the common good, or are at least have a semblance of control, then they will do incredible things. They will put up with atrocious working conditions just to be part of the endeavour. The famous 'red button experiment' of the 1960s exemplified this: on a production line employees were expected to repeat tedious tasks during 12-hour shifts. Morale was low. Productivity even lower. Employee turnover skyrocketed whenever other alternatives emerged for whatever job outside the factory. "Anything but this," people would say. However, the whole scenario was turned around with the installation of a red button on the production line. If something went wrong the employees could themselves halt the machines. Stop the press! They rarely pressed the red stop button, but the point was they felt they had a modicum of control. They were involved.

Empathy

Empathy is the third of the trio of EQ. Empathy as part of motivation is about sensing the mood of those around you and acting accordingly. It is about seeing the situation through their eyes, or at least attempting to do so. If you charge into meetings late and take no allowance for what has already been said, what's going on, who needs special attention, you are not leading or motivating and you will not achieve results. Situation sensing is a subtle touch that is generally learned not in the classroom, but in human interaction and relationships as we grow up.

Empathy is about acting and interacting with others according to their preferences. It is treating people the way they want to be treated, not treating them how you like to be treated. In the workplace, it is essential to try to understand what makes your team members tick. With critical feedback, for example. Some like feedback daily, hourly, given to them straight. They will have no problem doing this in front of everybody else. They just want to get it done, said, and they want to move on. Others like to schedule a chat behind closed doors. They may want details, facts, analysis. Others may want feedback casually, over coffee. It's all a question of gauging the preferences of your players and acting accordingly. Empathy is a key part of the required daily leadership activity of the Chief Wellbeing Officer and we will look at it again in chapter nine.

Emotional intelligence allows us to bring the humanity back to leadership – a call we made in chapter three. More tyrannical leaders may achieve results in the short-term, through fear, coercion, and pressure, but the best leaders practice a form of holistic leadership that gains results in the long-term. Emotional intelligence is an element of total intelligence that can be cultivated easily. Start practising better-quality conversations, listening, and spreading a message of common purpose that motivates others. Think of your own behaviours and the example you are setting. People actively look to be inspired, and a greater level of EQ will inspire those around you. With our heart set firmly in the right direction, let us now turn our attention to the body in the next chapter.

Communication, motivation, and empathy are cornerstones of the Montserrat school. In an increasingly connected world the missionary nuns look to encourage contact with schoolchildren around the world as a key facet of their learning methodology. This develops emotional intelligence in particular. A strategy of total intelligence influences the school day. Morning yoga practice by the nuns may be considered strange in some quarters, yet it is indicative of their belief in doing things differently and the need to disrupt the current education model that is failing our children.

6
LEADING
THROUGH
PHYSICAL
INTELLIGENCE

"You want to know how I did it? This is how I did it, Anton: I never saved anything for the swim back."

Vincent, *Gattaca*

THE BEST footballer in the world plays for FC Barcelona. Watching Leo Messi in full flight, especially at close quarters, is a sight to behold. Physical development is of course a key focus for any athlete, but it is development that didn't come easy to Messi. Suffering from growth hormone disorder as a child, he had to endure painful daily injections in each leg from the age of 11 until he was 14. His undoubted natural ability is the core of his astronomical physical intelligence (PQ), yet this was made more special through years of training and adversity which led to the resilient player we see today, in spite of his relevant lack of stature at 1.7m.

The second chapter of total intelligence focuses on PQ. If emotional intelligence (EQ) considers the leader as a human being, here we view the leader as an athlete. This does not mean we expect managers to become marathon runners. Our aim is to detail key factors, the critical behaviours we presented in chapter four, that undoubtedly affect performance in a business as well as sporting context. In the same way that EQ allows leadership to be sustainable through the long-term commitment and loyalty of the people around you, PQ also creates sustainable value, countering the dangers of neglecting the body, including sickness, stress, and burnout.

Leadership development rarely includes our physical selves, yet a growing body of research in different fields, from cardiology to neuroscience and biochemistry, emphasizes the clear link between the brain and the body. Deep insight in either of these two areas increasingly needs careful consideration of the other.

Notions of the physical self are present in different areas of management, from the established science on body language over the years, to the rapid rise and subsequent backlash in the space of embodied cognition theory (ECT) during 2016[1]. Though not the originator of the theory, Professor Amy Cuddy brought significant attention to ECT through her TED talk and research on 'power poses' – highlighting the importance of adopting expansive physical postures as a means of improving confidence. We are aware of the physical effect of some emotional states – for example, if we are tired or sad, there would be a corresponding physical manifestation of that state. Yet ECT contends that the opposite is true: if we adopt a particular physical state, there will be a corresponding emotional or mental effect. So sit up straight in that chair! Social Presencing Theater (SPT) has been used by author and MIT academic Otto Scharmer in his leadership interventions to think about workplace relationships and the example we set as leaders[2]. An SPT session is like a human sculpture in which people physically represent their organization, play themselves as individuals, and move in ways that represent workplace dynamics. The idea is to surface issues that are preventing high performance.

Our own work has been guided by considering behaviour and habits, reminding busy professionals that they have a body.

New behaviour which promotes movement and exercise may positively affect workplace dynamics, since the work environment will better support natural human behaviour. Simply put, it is a much more natural human trait to move and exercise than sit in a chair for eight-to-ten hours a day. Behavioural economics, psychology, wellbeing, and happiness are all areas of study here. The foundations of these benefits come from neuroscience and we now understand much more on the cognitive benefits of exercise, which we detail later in the chapter.

Sustaining Executive Performance (SEP)

The business case for multiple intelligence is something we developed in the Sustaining Executive Performance (SEP) programme. First created in 2007, SEP grew rapidly at Universitas Telefónica through delivery to all university attendees from 2012. It has been integrated in all programmes through short, practical sessions that look at areas including physical exercise, nutrition, sleep, and digital distraction, and specifically their link with the way of working. The main inspiration for SEP came from two main sources: the corporate athlete methodology, which showed that the physical self, and the sport domain (which relies on recovery and nutrition as well as physical development for performance) could offer valuable lessons for management. The work of Juliette and Michael McGannon on executive health, primarily at INSEAD, showed that such instruction had a place in management training. The result is that SEP has been delivered to over 20,000 managers around the world since 2010, including inclusion in executive education programmes at several of the world's leading business schools. The SEP book was published by Financial Times Pearson in 2014.[3]

Figure 6.1. The Sustaining Executive Performance (SEP) model

Two of the five elements of SEP consider the body and PQ directly: MOVE, which regards incidental movement in a normal professional day and the dangers of a sedentary life; and TRAIN, which considers dedicated physical exercise. Another two are traditionally used in sport to support performance of the body: RECOVER, in which sleep is a primary concern; and FUEL, which focuses on the role of nutrition in business. The FOCUS element, though not concerning our physical selves directly, includes concepts such as mindfulness, which in many ways starts with the body through increasing an awareness of our physical selves, breathing, and the connection between body and mind.

SEP considers some of our basic human needs that contribute to wellbeing and performance in the long-term. Executive health is often an oxymoron. That is the more executive a person is, the less health they normally enjoy! The performance case allows us to take a broader view of management life – towards true sustainable leadership – which has wellbeing at its core, and further allows us to challenge certain long-held management orthodoxies. What does a successful business career look like? Intention, resolution, and aspiration for starters. Bold objectives, ambitious plans and, perhaps, the fruits of achieving those targets? Reserved parking, chauffeur services and business-class air travel may help simplify an executive life in order to focus on the business at hand, yet therein dangers also lie for health, which ultimately drives that business performance.

Consider the following statements, representative of a typical 'successful' executive. To what extent do they apply to your life today?

1. Spending a large part of the day ensconced in an office behind a large desk.

2. Glorifying four hours' sleep. Being the first to arrive and last to leave.

3. Always online, busy, hyper-reactive, and multi-tasking.

4. Enjoying endless sumptuous business dinners. Mindless eating at home and work.

5. No time for, or legitimacy placed on, physical training.

We are realistic. Work is work, and from time to time our lives will represent part of the above profile, but we don't think this should be fully representative at all times. Sustainable business performance is built on the foundations of health, and this is driven by cultivating more movement, recovery, focus, attention to food as fuel, and training time.

And this is the good news. Executive health need not be about taking that near sabbatical from normal life to fit in training for next year's Ironman (although we see many of our alpha business leaders tackle such an undertaking with the same gusto as a grand business challenge). Admirable, yet perhaps not sustainable, and certainly not conducive to better business performance.

The far easier and more beneficial strategy for business performance is a change in mindset that comes from subtle behaviour change; new habits, routines, and ways of working. This is true for all elements of total intelligence and we take an in-depth look at the process of changing habits in chapter ten.

Changing the signs of managerial success may also create energy in the organization. When top executives have good habits, it motivates others. For example, all members of the C-suite of a top technology multinational that we've worked with no longer take the elevator. It may sound trite but it can make a big difference. Businesses should also realize that work is no longer about 'desktime', and allow their employees more flexibility and trust to get on with delivering the best results.

So what are some of the other subtle behaviour changes, new habits and ways of working you could change in your own life and implement in the organization? A brief summary of the five elements of SEP is included below, with a focus on content closely related to PQ.

1. Move

This element looks to cultivate more incidental movement in a sedentary life – it is not about finding time separate from work to move, rather how to integrate more dynamism within typical work practices that will improve both health and managerial performance. When we move we energize ourselves, through increased blood flow to the body and brain, and an increase in metabolism. This is our first law of SEP: that movement creates energy, not, as we tend to believe, spends our energy.

The current professional environment is characterized by a largely sedentary existence that has serious consequences for our health, wellbeing, mood, and productivity. On a simple level we are seated excessively, with *Harvard Business Review* noting that "sitting is the smoking of our generation".[4] This is due to the lack of awareness regarding the dangers of a sedentary life (as per tobacco pre-1960s) and for the effect that a sedentary life has on life expectancy, with research showing it to be similar as being a medium to heavy smoker. Forget about sky-diving then, having an office job may be one of the most dangerous things you can do!

We have designed and constructed a modern world in which movement is harder than ever. Yet there are significant business benefits of more mindful movement. Standing meetings, as practiced by many in the Agile programming field over the years, are much leaner and cut down the wasted time of poorly focused, overlong meetings that characterize much of the working week. Research by the *Wall Street Journal* and Harvard Business School found that 40% of a manager's week is spent in meetings. A standing desk, used by Ernest Hemingway when writing all his books, may help contribute to the three-to-four hours' daily standing time at work which gives the equivalent calorie burn of running ten marathons a year.[5]

Figure 6.2. Nudge poster from The Leadership Academy of Barcelona

Changing the design of a chair has been shown to improve brainstorming, with a more upright posture resulting in less criticism of the wild ideas necessary for innovation. Also in the creativity domain, a recent Stanford study found that walking improved creativity by an average of 60% compared to sitting[6] – so take that walking meeting. They are useful to build relationships, cover sensitive subjects, and drill down on a tough problem. Research has also shown that eliminating the chair altogether improves collaborative outcomes, with individuals less likely to defend their own territory. The conclusion was that when people had their own chair, it was a physical representation of defending their own point of view.

Finally, getting away from the desk has long been shown to result in more accidental encounters which drive innovation – a fact that is being reflected in the design of new office spaces by companies including Apple and Google. This is the movement imperative for business performance.

2. Recover

Recovery is valued as a key driver of performance in different fields such as sport. Yet in business it is largely ignored, with a machine-based view of work still prevalent in most organizations. That is, hard work in a linear, always-on fashion rather than responding to the oscillation of natural human rhythms. Work is work – we do not call for excessive breaks at the expense of getting things done, but point to the growing research and cases that show sustainable work performance is driven by an adequate attention to recovery.

The principal means of recovery is sleep, yet it may also include notions of break time, time outside, and in varying workspaces and tasks. Sleep has enjoyed a significant amount of attention in a business context over recent years. Even companies known for hard business cultures such as McKinsey and Accenture are turning their attention to the topic, making the call for sleep training for all managers in an organization and the installation of nap rooms respectively. A key message for a high-pressure environment where results are expected each day is that "a good day begins the night before".

It remains to be seen however the extent to which the culture of such organizations, as evidenced by the behaviours of the senior leaders and the hungry young associates who aspire to be them, actually changes. It certainly won't happen overnight.

3. Focus

Focus regards the ability to do quality work without distractions. Many of the societal and technological changes of the last ten years, principally due to the use of smartphones, are a significant source of these distractions, yet they may also come from a lack of a well-designed workspace or operations that prevent people getting quality work done. Our brains are serial processors, which means that multitasking is impossible, at least without the likelihood of making errors and/or increasing task time.

For any organization, consideration should be given to the high-quality, focused work that needs to be completed with accuracy, and the means by which that may be protected. Certain staff need to be reactive and on-call, yet recognizing that two different types of work exist, and that distractions can cause stress as well as error is important. On a simple level, are there enough workspace options that support private, focussed work? We will look at such questions in depth in chapter 11 on environmental design.

4. Fuel

What, when, and how we eat can affect our energy, mood, and decisions. Simple fluctuations in blood sugar can affect all of the above and can be easily remedied. A comprehensive view on available eating choices in and around the workplace, kitchen design (if appropriate), and eating areas for employees is increasingly required in the competitive workplace of today.

Eating while travelling is an area of specific difficulty we find in our executive coaching. Being hostage to the food available at an airport, train station, or petrol station can lead to a spiral of poor eating choices, compromised business decision-making, and weight gain. When we are tired or stressed (frequent companions during travel) we often make a beeline for processed starchy carbohydrates, high glycemic index foods which give us an instant boost through the rapid release of glucose into our bloodstream, but which leads to a cycle of spiking and crashing our blood sugar. Witness the behavioural changes in children after the consumption of sugar to realize that adult decisions could easily be affected too. Weight is gained through the surging of insulin which is stored as fat.

A simple remedy relates to a basic understanding of human anatomy: the size of our stomach is approximately the size of our fist, though a little longer. It stretches of course, yet this tells us that we can achieve satiety by snacking on an amount of food that fills the palm of our hand, such as nuts and dried fruit. Travelling with a 'survival pack' will therefore get you through the sticky moments of the journey until you reach a destination where a broader, healthier menu is available.

5. Train

Whereas MOVE regards incidental movement as part of a professional day, TRAIN looks at dedicated physical exercise. We consider how to legitimize and then integrate athletic training in a busy professional life.

How do you fit exercise into your life? Is it best to exercise before going to work, rising early as many busy executives do? Try and fit it in (and therefore benefit from the energy boost) in the middle of the day? Or wait until the end of the day after the core block of work has been completed? The choice will depend on the individual. We see most going for the early morning option but see massive potential in the middle of the day, and view this as being more common in the future as companies loosen their out-dated adherence to nine-to-five desktime.

As with the FUEL element, a consideration of dedicated physical exercise while travelling may be useful, with the tips noted below also useful for home. The key to exercising on the road often relates to hotel planning before the trip, and it's not what you think. The three elements of executive fitness – incidental movement, aerobic (heart-rate) intensity, and strength-based exercise – can be achieved by not stepping near the hotel gym.

When booking a hotel, we advise looking for a multistorey building of at least seven storeys. Even if you only have ten minutes available, it is possible to complete a high-intensity interval session in the stairwell of the hotel, sprinting to the top before jogging back down. Such a session may be completed at a lower intensity or take into account a lower level of fitness by walking up and walking down. The heart rate will exhibit the same high and low rhythms as for any interval session. Stairs are gold-dust for the busy professional. As well as offering an easy opportunity to work on aerobic fitness and core strength, they offer a welcome mental break from the office environment.

Strength-based work is often the safest and most valuable when using one's own body weight. No matter how small the hotel room, easy-to-do exercises such as planks are a small time commitment with big gain (try three sets of ten seconds in plank position with, five seconds recovery in between). The seven-minute workout, first developed by exercise physiologist Chris Jordan at the Johnson & Johnson Human Performance Institute, may also be easily completed within the confines of a hotel room and there are now many apps available to help guide this.

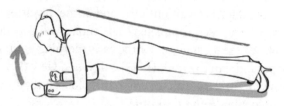

Figure 6.3. Holding the plank position

A final consideration for business travel is a suspension trainer, like a TRX. This is composed of two durable nylon straps that fit easily in a small bag and can be hung on the inside of a door to do a variety of body-weight exercises. Just remember to lock the door and put on the do-not-disturb sign!

The Sustaining Executive Performance model therefore takes many of the elements of the multiple intelligence view and makes them usable within the working environment. We see such behaviours as becoming part of the standard toolkit or basic managerial competence in the future. Indeed, many of the millennial generation already integrate some of these behaviours as a matter of course.

What is your own daily professional reality according to these five dimensions? We're realistic, we don't expect you to focus on maximizing all five at all times. Indeed, the best approach is to think about what you need at a specific time according to the professional context. For example, would exercise really be required at the end of a long day travelling, even if that travel was highly sedentary? Perhaps a short meditation, then getting to bed would be more beneficial. Use the following checklist as a reflection on daily habits within your normal working environment rather than an iron-clad prescription for new behaviour.

Table 6.1. Journey to the sustainable Leader

	Ticking Time-Bomb!	Urgent Change Still Required	Not the Worst, but Who Wants to be Average?	Good, go for Great!		The Sustainable Leader
Move	1 I'm always sitting down – sofa, car, office – and I don't have many opportunities to walk during the day.	2	3	4	5	I don't stop. I rarely sit down and have a good level of energy throughout the day.
Recover	1 I don't sleep well, always waking up tired and going through my day feeling stressed and without time to take a break.	2	3	4	5	I sleep around eight high-quality hours each night. I know how to escape from the chaos that might ensue if required.
Focus	1 My day is full of distractions. I'm always online and feel like I have no time to do quality thinking.	2	3	4	5	I can disconnect from my smartphone and computer without feeling anxious, and am generally in control of my various devices.
Fuel	1 I simply eat what is in front of me. I have no time for breakfast, or a good lunch. I tend to snack often during the day.	2	3	4	5	I'm very aware of all my meal choices and the process of eating. I often prepare meals myself and think about the energy they give me.
Train	1 I don't have time to exercise. It's a luxury I can't afford.	2	3	4	5	I always have a minimum three days a week with dedicated physical exercise. I know how to fit it in within a demanding professional schedule.

The neuroscience of PQ

The language and inner working of the brain isn't an easy concept to grasp, but we aim to provide an overview of the main brain benefits through exercise here. As we age, the brain suffers a dynamic process of remodelling, which is known as neuroplasticity. This term refers to the capacity of the brain to change and reorganize in response to the environment – for example, during the learning process. The hippocampus, one of the main areas of the brain involved in learning and memory processes, has an important degree of neuroplasticity. When these processes are impaired in the hippocampus, different neurodegenerative illnesses, such as Alzheimer's, and psychiatric disorders like schizophrenia or severe depression, may result. Research shows that aerobic exercise is one of the most effective lifestyle factors, often proving more effective than prescription drugs, to boost neuroplasticity in the hippocampus, and generally improve cognitive performance.

These studies show that exercise programmes of between three and 12 months improve cognitive status – including attention, executive function, processing speed, motor functioning, and memory – not only in healthy, young and middle-aged adults, but also for older cohorts and even in people with mild cognitive impairments or dementia. A regular exercise routine or programme is a key consideration. Research also shows that the executive function benefits accrued from exercise tend to dissipate 48 hours after the session. To clarify, executive function tasks are those cognitive functions including reasoning, problem solving, and planning, which though not exclusive to managers, will comprise daily managerial activity.

Coming back to the brain plasticity mechanisms supported by exercise, it is established that the benefits for cognition are grouped in direct and indirect effects. Regarding indirect effects, these are related to an improvement of health status, such as stress and sleep, together with a reduction of chronic diseases like coronary heart diseases and metabolic syndrome. Direct effects have been described in animal studies (mainly in rodents, though not super-rats!), which involve a stimulation of three distinct processes in the hippocampus: neurogenesis, synaptogenesis, and angiogenesis[7-10], described below.

1. Neurogenesis refers to the process of forming new neurons in the adult brain, relating to the dentate gyrus of the hippocampus as being one of the two brain regions where neurogenesis occurs. Studies in rodents shows that neurogenesis stimulation by exercise leads to an improvement of performance in memory tests.

2. Regarding synaptogenesis, this term involves the changes that take place in the synapses of the neurons, where aerobic exercise increases length, complexity, and spine density in the hippocampus. These changes induce higher rates of long-term potentiation, which refers to a strengthening of synaptic connections between neurons, boosting improvements in cognition.

3. Finally angiogenesis, or the formation of new capillaries, increases cerebral blood flow in the hippocampus, which means a greater supply of oxygen and glucose. This increased blood flow also stimulates both neurogenesis and synaptogenesis.

Memory, general cognitive performance, as well as increased creativity and problem-solving that we may infer from a greater supply of oxygen and glucose are therefore some of the direct cerebral benefits gained by exercise.

Our biochemistry, which we consider further in chapter eight, reveals further benefits. Brain-derived neurotrophic factor (BDNF) is the most important protein generated by exercise, where higher levels are observed in human serum after exercise. BDNF also modulates energy metabolism and strengthens the synaptic connections between neurons. Vascular endothelial-derived growth factor (VEGF) and insulin growth factor 1 (IGF-1) are the other main proteins generated by exercise that support the above hippocampal processes. BDNF is also one of the main proteins generated by good sleep.

Aerobic exercise therefore has a key role in the performance of our brain. Much of the research has considered healthy ageing, with for example, cognitive reserve considering the protective effects against dementia and other brain disorders in older people who maintained higher levels of activity through their lives. However, other emerging areas (including learning efficacy for children) consider how we may become our best selves now through considering more of the physical dimension.

Building the right culture of PQ

The British distance runner Brendan Foster was once asked by an awed reporter what it felt like to be an Olympian. The reporter was clearly expecting some form of superhuman sensation – certainly not the fact that Foster was "tired... tired all the time". Taking physical effort to the extreme will not allow the balance required for us to operate at our best on both a physical and intellectual level. A call for such balance can be traced back to the origins of the Olympics. The Greek philosopher Plato would lecture on the virtues of physical education, and the body-mind balance, with the goal to "bring the two elements into tune with one another by adjusting the tension of each to the right pitch". Just as much a danger as neglecting the body, focusing only on the body to the detriment of this balance would result in athletes becoming unadaptable and sluggish, needing too much sleep.

A culture where people are empowered to move freely and defy the conventions of management orthodoxy, including sitting at their desks all day as a sign of 'getting stuff done' is required.

A subtle approach to the physical dimension is therefore required in the workplace. Design of the physical environment will help, as we detail in chapter 11, together with leaders serving as good examples through their behaviour. A culture where people are empowered to move freely and defy the conventions of management orthodoxy, including sitting at their desks all day as a sign of 'getting stuff done' is required. This is especially important, as people may feel alienated if they are currently out of shape or have never experienced much physical activity. Like Messi, most of us will have to contend with physical limitations to be our best, but therein also lies the value in PQ for leadership.

Some business professionals also suffer from a PQ data obsession. Wearable technology companies aim to incentivize the user and lock-in use of their products. Gaining a badge for 10,000 steps walked in a day is a positive feature. But what follows? Badges for 15,000, 20,000 and more. We're then encouraged to spend our lives collecting badges rather than being more mindful of movement and relating that to other physical and mental factors in our professional day. For example, was I more energized as a result of walking 10,000 steps? Was my decision-making and creativity better or worse? The causal relationship should therefore be the focus, not the data in itself.

This is where we see an opportunity for managers to integrate notions of the physical self in an effective and sustainable manner. Reflection on practice and measurement are hallmarks of good management. As managers we are surrounded by a menagerie of metrics – customer churn, employee turnover, operational capacity, and countless others – in an attempt to increase company competitiveness. We are experts in examining the processes whereby different variables have different effects. Athletes too are experts in this process, with a view to maximizing their personal athletic performance.

Sport, like many other areas of modern society, has undergone a technological revolution, yet one of the most valuable tools for an athlete remains the training diary. Having a diary where one can reflect, add notes on physical and mental states, the weather, opponents, and of course the quantitative stuff – kilometres, seconds, centimetres – is the data on which progress and motivation is based. This is why tracking can be so powerful. Progress is fuel. It is the energy for continuing with practice. Transferring this to the professional domain, a training diary is recommended, or perhaps it is just called an executive journal. Studies have shown that keeping a journal has major mental health benefits for the modern-day professional. It allows us to be more mindful and offers a pause (normally at the end of the day) to reflect, be grateful, and think about where we've been and where we're going.

Peter Drucker famously said that "we can't manage what we can't measure". In a long, productive career, which Drucker himself acknowledged to now last 50 years or more, the physical self can no longer be separate from traditional notions of an executive life.

The career of an athlete is nowhere near as long. Messi is closer now to the end of his career than the beginning, with ever-closer attention paid to data collection, cause and effect, behaviour and culture in order to reap the benefits of his PQ for as long as possible. In the same way that PQ ought to be a vital part of leadership development, it should not be the only element in athletic development. Entering FC Barcelona's La Masia football academy as a 13-year-old, Messi was introduced to a methodology that nurtures the intellectual and social development of the children they have in their care. Part of the reason for doing so is recognizing their responsibility, as many of the academy students will not progress to a professional career. Yet there is also a strong belief that the development of other facets of these young human beings will improve their footballing ability. Total intelligence – for sport, business, and life – is the cornerstone of our improved wellbeing.

7
LEARNING TO LIVE

"Do not go gentle into that good night. Old age should burn and rave at close of day. Rage, rage against the dying of the light."

Dr. Brand, *Interstellar*

THEY said he was an idiot. They said his sketches were infantile and that it looked like a child had done them. They were right! He did paint like a child as an adult, but more interestingly he had painted like a master when he was a mere child. Pablo Picasso was a genius. He was born in Malaga in the south of Spain in 1881 and his family moved to Barcelona when he was five, where he stayed for the next 20 years, before he left for France. He said of Barcelona "There is where it all began... where I understood how far I could go."

This chapter is about learning to survive, and thrive, in a sea of change. By better understanding the great waves of change, we can learn to be masters of disruption, rather than victims. This is true on an individual and organizational level, and we will show how the Chief Wellbeing Officer can ask the right questions to help both the person and company navigate safely and successfully.

The very essence of wellbeing is finding, and acting according to, your authentic self. It is easy to lose sight of our authenticity due to a variety of factors, life experiences, bad habits, poor choices, and the environment in which we spend most of our time. We may even achieve a great deal of success acting inauthentically, though if that success does last, it is unlikely to be fulfilling. Exposing ourselves to outside points of view and influences is healthy, as is learning from others and getting new ideas, but we must always stay true to who we are. As Oscar Wilde said, "Be yourself, everybody else is already taken." This quest for authenticity builds on our discussion in chapter three on defining purpose, values, and vision, and we will enrich that quest through different means in this chapter, including a call to adopt a more childlike mindset.

First, let us turn our attention to understanding those large waves of change.

The curves of change

The S-curve first appeared in 1962 as part of Professor Everett Rogers' work on the diffusion of innovation.[1] He specifically looked at how and why ideas and products spread through different cultures, giving rise to the well-known bell-curve distribution or life-cycle, with the S-curve being the cumulative plot of the life-cycle as shown below.

By better understanding the great waves of change, we can learn to be masters of disruption, rather than victims.

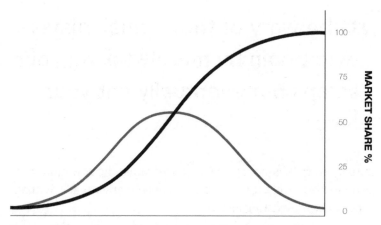

Figure 7.1. Understanding market diffusion as an S-curve

In 1986, McKinsey & Company director Richard Foster then used the S-curve to describe how the performance of a technology varies over time, or more strictly, how it varies with increased research and development effort or investment.[2] Technological performance increases with effort but eventually hits an upper limit or plateau, where further improvement would either be impossible or prohibitively expensive. To achieve higher performance requires a discontinuous switch to a different technology, in turn following its own S-curve. The new S-curve may start at a performance level below the old one but has potential to overtake its predecessor.

This thinking really caught the mainstream with Harvard Business School Professor Clayton Christensen's book on *The Innovator's Dilemma,* in which he stated that all companies, no matter how successful, must at some point leave behind the old way of doing things and make the switch to a new path. Even if that new path is seemingly of no value, in terms of both market and performance, it will have the potential to eventually overtake the existing solution. Technological disruption therefore occurs when an innovation emerges that offers superior performance along a new dimension, even if performance on conventional measures is

So be wary of those small players who begin by merely taking your scraps but eventually eat your lunch.

initially poor. Incumbents will tend to dismiss the new innovation as no importance, yet it may create a new market that eventually supersedes the existing one.

This isn't easy to do. Companies become big and arrogant, and are blind to what will create value in the future. As an example, let's look at Kodak, the Google of its day. Up until 1990 it was regularly classified as one of the top-five highest-value brands in the world, with $2.5 billion in revenues and 145,000 employees by 1999. It still exists today, but is a mere shadow of its former self, having missed the transition to digital photography. Yet it had all the know-how for survival as one of its engineers, Steven Sasson, actually invented the digital camera. Forty years ago, he went to his boss and presented his invention. It weighed four kilos and the quality of the images was 0.01 megapixels. The image was stored in a cassette. His boss laughed, in fact everybody laughed at him, and he despondently went back to his lab. The rest is history, as digital photography killed film, and then smartphones killed the camera. These steps are no more than a series of disruptions that could have been foreseen. In a similar vein let's not forget that Microsoft invented the tablet computer and Nokia the tactile screen. So be wary of those small players who begin by merely taking your scraps but eventually eat your lunch.

In recent years, the S-curve has been used as a lens to understand change in different fields in science and business, including personal disruption. It is not a scientific reality, rather a useful framework to surface the right questions.

Our belief therefore, akin to Christensen's dilemma for companies is that all people, no matter how successful, must at some point leave behind the old way of doing things and make the switch to a new path

A case from Professor MacGregor

Disruption is not new. Let's consider change at the level of a whole industry. Perhaps the world's oldest is the spice trade or Silk Roads, essentially one and the same thing. For thousands of years there was two-way trade from the Far East and great empires of China to Western Europe, and later to the Americas. Silk and spices like cardamom, cinnamon, and pepper as well as horses and slaves would flow in both directions. Millions of people were employed, from peasant farmers growing the products, local merchants buying and transporting, port authorities, ships, then buyers at the other end, shops, more merchants, and end users. The value chain was immense.

For three thousand years this trade endured, with Venice becoming the capital from about 1100 to 1500. Companies like the Dutch East India Company grew so large and rich that they acted like nations. They had more than a million employees, a fleet of ships more impressive than almost any nation's armada, powers to invade countries, and even to execute employees when they desired. Then, in the space of a few years all this came to an end. The mighty industry became a mere shadow of what it had once been.

Frederic Tudor became known as the Boston Ice King in around 1850. He disrupted the whole spice trade, not by inventing better ships or better routes, but by developing another method of conserving food. That, after all, was the core purpose of the spice trade. Its purpose was about food preservation. Tudor developed a whole new sector that produced ice in New England: he would establish great ice fields in large lakes that would be cut and harvested into ice blocks. The ice blocks would be stored in large warehouses. Despite the lack of modern refrigeration, the thermodynamic properties of ice meant that only a few millimetres of ice would melt each day. From the warehouses, the ice would then be transported to houses.

Most middle-class families had an ice box and received a delivery twice a week. This was the modern way to preserve food and the spice trade became obsolete. How many of the players in the spice trade made it into the ice trade? How many of those peasant farmers, shippers, and traders managed to adapt to the new reality? Zero!

Then John Gorrie invented the artificial ice machine. A bit like the first digital camera, it was big, expensive, and difficult to use. The incumbent, Babson, with his lakes and massive production network could not imagine that it was a threat. He laughed. They all scoffed. He said it was impractical. He was making the classic mistake of every big, comfortable high-end business: arrogance and complacency.

By 1910 everybody had a refrigerator and the ice business was gone. How many people in the ice trade made it into the world of artificial refrigeration? Zero! Even the ships were not equipped to ship fridges, they were set up for ice blocks.

Will we enter a post-refrigerator phase? Who knows. Perhaps food that doesn't need refrigeration. Or maybe Amazon, with its one-hour delivery, its sophisticated network of suppliers and couriers, and drones will render it all obsolete.

Figure 7.2. A 19th-century ice-delivery man

Disrupt yourself

Disruption is the natural order of life – where change, death, and rebirth are ever-present. By better understanding the main rhythms and their transitions, we may take advantage on both a personal and business level.

So what are those main rhythms? First, everything has a beginning, and then it grows. It grows at varying rates until eventually reaching a plateau or maturity, after which it will start to decline and eventually die. The key is to understand the point at which decline begins, understand the signs around you, and instead of being tied to the decline, follow the new growth path. This is the moment of disruption. You have disrupted the natural course of events.

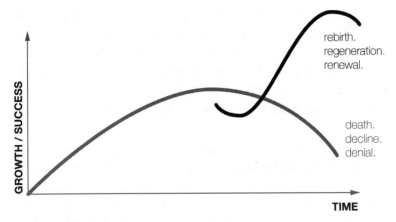

Figure 7.3. The life-cycle of growth

The big challenge, apart from being aware of what is going on around you, is that in order to jump to a new curve you have to pass through a period of chaos. This is a difficult time. Opportunity is high, but so is fear. If the curve represents you, or your career, this is a very tiring time. This difficulty can be attributed to two main factors. First, there is a high degree of ambiguity. This is good in the long-run, since ambiguity and the lack of rushing to definition is what opens up a whole world of new opportunities. Yet ambiguity is not a naturally acceptable concept for us as human beings. Second, as originally detailed by Foster in his technology S-curves, is that the new curve will start at a level of performance lower than the existing path. This can be a difficult reality for us to grasp – that in order to go forward in the long-run, we must first go backwards. The transition may be likened in part to the productive zone of disequilibrium developed as part of the adaptive leadership field. There is enough tension to change for the better, embracing different possibilities, yet ideally not so much tension that fear takes hold to the detriment of positive change.

Leadership is about establishing the context around you and then moving towards actions (making choices). The chaos stage is one where it is essential to hold the pressure of everything that is swirling around you. You must establish all the options, read the signs, see the massive opportunities, but don't jump too soon, nor prevaricate and wait too long. Jumping too soon or waiting too long may cause you to miss the opportunity of the new path, the new curve, and you will head towards inevitable decline.

In addition to the new curve starting at a lower performance level, the S-curve shape also dictates that progress will be slow initially. It may seem that nothing is happening despite the momentous actions you have taken in order to get there. Be patient and be sure that things will pick up and may move into fast growth that is represented by the steep part of the curve. Hold the course and don't fall into the temptation of old habits that represent your former self.

Understanding where you are now allows us to move forward. Are you in A, B, C or D for your personal life and career or company product or strategy?

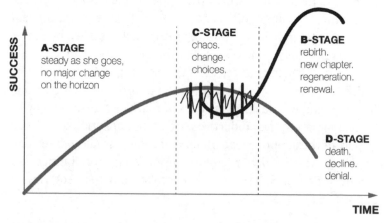

Figure 7.4. The life-cycle of growth, with stages A to D

Start by listening to the conversations around you. For example, if you are using the model to analyze the life-cycle of a company product, the things people are talking about are growth, production and marketing. If in B you will feel a lot of energy and new ideas around you. In C there is a constant battle for resources. The company may be panicking a little and throwing more and more KPIs at the situation. Fear may be tangible. At D there is only talk of cost cutting, and the employees are all hiding and waiting for Friday.

Apply this same logic to your personal life and wellbeing. Be clear on what stage you are in and make choices. If you are at A, the main thing is to stay the course, do more of what you are already doing. If you are at B, be patient and ensure you don't slip back to C. Growth will come. At C it is about holding down all the pressure, assessing opportunities, and considering where you are going to focus. D may simply involve a hard stop, cutting your losses and moving on, even if this is painful. For example, this may involve divorce or quitting your job.

How can you be sure where you are, or that the new path really is the one to follow? Hindsight is a wonderful thing and there are certainly examples of killing a successful product too soon. We would advise two things: first, listen to your heart. Truly listen. Get away from your daily distractions and reconnect with your authentic self. You will often find the answer there. Second, listen to others. Who do you trust and who could give you a more dispassionate view on the situation?

Jumping too soon or waiting too long may cause you to miss the opportunity of the new path, the new curve, and you will head towards inevitable decline.

TRY THE FOLLOWING EXERCISE TO RECONNECT WITH YOUR AUTHENTIC SELF AS A MEANS OF BETTER RIDING THE WAVES OF DISRUPTION

Our past reveals rich insights for wellbeing to thrive, yet is often hidden and hard to uncover. There may be things you do not want to relive, but by acknowledging them we may move forward as a more resilient being.

Association is a powerful means of uncovering the past. The way we sense things and how that makes us feel leaves a very definite mark on our subconscious. Consider the sense of smell, perhaps a grandmother's recipe that, when sensed again, transports you immediately back to your childhood. It's like Proust and his madeleine in *In Search of Lost Time*. He dips his madeleine cake into a cup of tea, he smells something he has not smelled for years and it evokes something deep. A stream of consciousness is unleashed. The past had been hidden and forgotten but he manages to rekindle it. He realizes he can learn from it and understand what all those past memories, "lying dormant, poised like souls waiting and hoping for their moment," say about his true self.

Music is another powerful association. *Desert Island Discs* is a radio programme broadcast by the BBC since the 1940s and is one of the world's longest-running radio shows. Each week a guest, called a 'castaway', is asked to choose eight recordings (usually, but not always, music), a book and a luxury item they would take if they were to be cast away on a desert island, while discussing their lives and the reasons for their choices. More than 3,000 episodes have been recorded and there is a long, comprehensive archive of interesting podcasts to enjoy. Guests invariably come to the show thinking it will be easy but leave crying, such is the emotion that is unleashed through hidden memories. The music acts like Proust's madeleine.

So, begin by thinking about your young life as a child. Consider the early years, perhaps blissful and cared for deeply or experiencing hardship and neglect. Whatever it was, try to think of some music – maybe it's your earliest memories of music, maybe it's a lullaby your mother sang, or a song your father always played. Try to pinpoint it and savour the flavour of the music as it washes over you.

Next, think about your teens. Rebellion perhaps? Peer pressure at school? Consider what music defined you then. Perhaps you remember the first record or disc you bought. Find the music, play it and see how you feel. See if you are transported back to those teen years.

Then into your late teens and twenties. Maybe your first deep relationship. Maybe you made a mix tape for your boyfriend/ girlfriend. Maybe there was a break up and you were sad. What music comes to mind? Play it and remember.

Continue to do this until you have eight songs.

Play the songs and enjoy the unleashing of long-lost memories. Remember your behaviours in times of challenge, success, and failure. Remember how it felt to win or lose or feel excluded from a group, or to be on the wrong end of a break-up. In this way you are putting meat on the skeleton of your life. You are discovering you.

"And once I had recognized the taste of the crumb of madeleine soaked in her decoction of lime-flowers which my aunt used to give me (although I did not yet know and must long postpone the discovery of why this memory made me so happy), immediately the old grey house upon the street, where her room was, rose up like the scenery of a theatre to attach itself to the little pavilion, opening on to the garden, which had been built out behind it for my parents (the isolated panel which until that moment had been all that I could see); and with the house the town, from morning to night and in all weathers, the square where I was sent before luncheon, the streets along which I used to run errands, the country roads we took when it was fine… so in that moment all the flowers in our garden … and the water-lilies on the Vivonne and the good folk of the village and their little dwellings and the parish church and the whole of Combray and of its surroundings, taking their proper shapes and growing solid, sprang into being, town and gardens alike, all from my cup of tea."

In Search of Lost Time (vol 1), Marcel Proust, 1913

Bring out the child in you and your organization

The *Desert Island Discs* exercise is a powerful tool that shows the cycles of our lives. It is not uncommon to see things repeat themselves, say, every seven or so years. We may see success and failure through that time – a series of S-curves.

Reinvention is becoming a child again, curious to learn and adopt a beginner's mindset that is characterized by curiosity, exploration, and discovery. We all know how to make friends without starting with assumptions and judgments. We did that in the school playground. We all know how to openly express ourselves without fear of humiliation. Young children do that all the time. Yet over time our innate, authentic, and unique characteristics are eroded and moulded into a standardisation of what society or our family or company wants us to look like. During this process we lose the invaluable and naive ability to create, innovate, and be our authentic selves. Picasso said: "Every child is an artist... and then they grow up."

The childlike characteristics so often stolen from us as we grow, mature, and learn to socialize are exactly what so many companies are now asking for in their people: the ability to think out of the box, to think for themselves and innovate. Children are predisposed to authenticity and optimism. These are probably the two most important leadership characteristics that companies are crying out for, yet we humiliate our employees for displaying them.

All kids have incredible talents and then we ruthlessly squander them. As the famous educator and TED speaker Ken Robinson said, "Schools teach us literacy but kill creativity." He goes on to tell the story of the kindergarten teacher who was observing her classroom of children while they drew pictures. Occasionally, she would walk around the room to see each child's work. "What are you drawing?" she asked one little girl who was working diligently at her desk. The girl replied, "I'm drawing God." The teacher paused and said, "But no one knows what God looks like." The little girl replied, "They will in a minute."

This is what companies are missing, yet they consistently go out to destroy this childlike free-thinking attitude. It was said recently that "companies are abattoirs of the human soul". Companies step into our lives, just after we have been through years of training and conditioning by schools, and they keep on transforming us into the best version for them, again eroding our personal characteristics. At the same time they increasingly ask for creativity and passion. Yet wellbeing and the creativity, passion, and performance that comes from it, thrives when we reconnect with our authentic selves. This is what *Chief Wellbeing Officer* is here for, and there are signs that organizations are beginning to change. Microsoft CEO Satya Nadella talked in 2017 of his admiration for the book *MindSet* by Stanford professor Carol Dweck:

> "I was reading it not in the context of business or work culture, but in the context of my children's education. The author describes the simple metaphor of kids at school. One of them is a 'know-it-all' and other is a 'learn-it-all', and the learn-it-all always will do better than the other one, even if the know-it-all kid starts with much more innate capability. Going back to business: if that applies to boys and girls at school, I think it also applies to CEOs, like me, and entire organizations, like Microsoft. We want to be not a know-it-all but learn-it-all organization."

Such a learn-it-all approach is often held up as good practice in parenting, where the focus should not be on giving the answer to questions that children may have, but taking an approach of "let's find out together", in order to awaken interest in the process of discovery. The process and thirst for the answer is actually more important than the answer itself. Such a skill will be even more important for the complex problems of the future where there may not be a single answer. The way of thinking is more important, which can be deployed today to question why things exist in the organization, not simply because that's "the way it has always been done".

The energies of the Chief Wellbeing Officer may therefore be directed also to organizational health, ensuring that the company may thrive in the longer-term in spite of disruption and complexity. Responsible stewardship of the company involves navigating the rhythms of change outlined in this chapter. Testament to the great challenges of a disruptive age is the decreasing lifespan of a company: only half of the companies listed in the 1980 Fortune 500 still exist today, with a 15-year-old company now often perceived as old. As leading management academic Gary Hamel said, "Out there in some garage is an entrepreneur who's forging a bullet with your company's name on it." Once-mighty brands including Kodak, Blockbuster, Borders, and TWA were felled by such bullets.

In contrast, companies including Apple, IBM, Lego, Disney, and Fuji all survived near-death experiences to successfully reinvent themselves, following different iterations of the S-curve. They adapted and survived by asking the right questions, by being open to change, and by avoiding complacency and taking the right risks.

One of the main things about disruption is that it is difficult to see it coming. Especially if you are doing well in your business, have achieved market dominance, and all your KPIs look good – as they did for Kodak in 1999. It is therefore hard to imagine that you are under imminent threat of disappearance – yet is has now happened to so many companies in recent years.

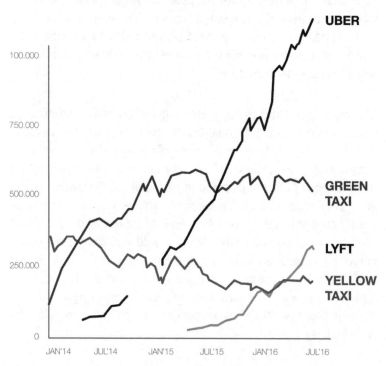

BROOKLYN MONTHLY TAXI PICKUPS

Figure 7.5. This is what disruption looks like, adapted from Analyzing *1.1 Billion NYC Taxi and Uber Trips, with a Vengeance* by Todd W. Schneider (toddwschneider.com)

The Chief Wellbeing Officer listens, asks questions internally and externally, has their eyes open, and might just sense a disruption on the horizon to enable the company to be part of it, rather than a victim. At the very least, organizations need to have the right childlike mindset prevalent within their employees so as to be able to move quickly when the need arises.

Picasso said that his abstraction was "the elimination of the unnecessary". This is the true concept of complex simplicity:

adult complexity with childlike simplicity. Just because the image Picasso created seems simplistic, does not mean it is not fiendishly sophisticated. The thing about abstraction is that it's ridiculously difficult, since it demands that you have a grasp of the underlying principles of what's going on. You have to ensure that every single line, every dot on the canvas, that every detail has a purpose. Picasso said that you have to begin with concrete reality and then, through simplicity-seeking abstraction, you remove traces of that reality. Given that you started with something real it shall always be in there. The idea of the object will have left an indelible mark. His visual essay on bull figures is the perfect example. The first few are hooved, horned, fleshy, and bull-like. The last one is just six lines and some shading, but it is just as lifelike. It hasn't lost any of its its 'bullness'. Steve Jobs said that "simple can be harder than complex. You have to work hard to get your thinking clean to make it simple. But it's worth it in the end because once you get there, you can move mountains."

Figure 7.6. Picasso's bulls by Ferran Bruguera

Can you simplify? Are you able to focus? This makes you more, not less, because you are not diluting yourself with things that are not important to you and your authentic self. Learning to live has two distinct meanings. First, in a longer life and career we must better navigate the waves of change and so we better learn how life unfolds. Second, on the role of learning *in order to* live. Learning is a never-ending process. Picasso also said, "I am always doing that which I cannot do, in order that I may learn how to do it." It seems he was a learn-it-all, too.

8

A DAY IN THE LIFE

"Well, good morning everybody, and welcome to day 255,642 aboard the *Axiom*. As always, the weather is a balmy 72 degrees and sunny."

The Captain, *WALL-E*

ALL CATALANS have constant jetlag. Barcelona time should be the same as London time. Go ahead, look at both cities on the world map. Indeed, Madrid is even further west on the solar longitude scale and west of the Greenwich Meridian. The country owes its present position in Central European Time to a political construct, and specifically the Spanish military dictator Francisco Franco. In 1940 he moved the clocks forward one hour in solidarity with Nazi Germany. For Spaniards still recovering from the devastation of the Civil War, complaining about the time was the last thing on their minds. So they continued to eat at the same time, and 1pm lunches became 2pm lunches, with 8pm dinners at 9pm. To this day, primetime TV is an unusually late hour for a European country. The working day finishes late and sleep-deprived children don't get to bed early enough, since they wait up until their parents are home.

The American author John C. Maxwell said that "you will never change your life until you change something you do daily". After reflecting on the patterns and rhythms that make up our lifelong learning journey in the last chapter, here we look at the patterns and rhythms of our daily life, allowing us to ground some of these bigger issues as we move towards the action part of *Chief Wellbeing Officer*.

We believe the professional day to be the key unit of analysis in understanding deeply our working lives. The de facto view in business is often on the business quarter or financial year, maybe even the five-year-plan, but the big picture and the bold aims and objectives contained within it are built on the success of the small stuff. In the Fourth Industrial Revolution, looking at the biological and social patterns of our day will allow us to retain and nurture the human element that is required for workplace wellbeing. Yet what are some of the origins of daily labour within our life? Looking at a seminal moment in the First Industrial Revolution offers some insight.

Balancing work and life

The first nursery school in the world was founded in 1816 by a Welshman in a Scottish cotton mill, among a series of pioneering initiatives that improved working conditions and even workers' diets. Robert Owen's management of the New Lanark mills from the year 1800 transformed the lives of the 2,000 people who lived an worked there, including 500 children, at the same time as delivering commercial success. Though New Lanark is held up as one of the model cases of socialist utopianism, some believe Owen acted as an enlightened capitalist, given his approach to balancing work and life for true progress in both areas. His approach to nursery education showcased such enlightenment: starting the day with dancing and singing, a classroom designed with high ceilings and natural sunlight, instruction outside when weather permitted, and a pedagogical focus on a world view and individual exploration are closer to innovative schools today rather than Victorian-era drudgery.

New Lanark became celebrated throughout Europe, and many leading royals, statesmen, and reformers visited the mills. In contrast with the normal working conditions of the day, they found a clean and healthy environment with a happy workforce that did not compromise a prosperous business. The work of Owen highlighted the human factor at a time when the First Industrial Revolution was treating people like machines. Rapid industrial progress resulted in the widespread adoption of a sun-up-to-sun-down workday, with many children foregoing their education to satisfy the demand for resources.

Owen first implemented a ten-hour day at the New Lanark mills and would later advocate an eight-hour workday as part of a balanced daily life that would include "eight hours' labour, eight hours' recreation, and eight hours' rest", and which would form the focus of the International Workers' Day or Labour Day holiday on 1 May.

Figure 8.1. Robert Owen's 'Triple 8'

One of the first businesses in the United States to implement Owen's eight-hour day was the Ford Motor Company. In 1914, it not only cut the standard workday to eight hours, but it also doubled its workers' pay in the process. To the shock of many at the time, this resulted in a significant increase in productivity, and Ford's profit margins doubled within two years of implementation. This encouraged other companies to adopt the shorter eight-hour workday as a standard for their employees.

So does Owen's 'Triple 8' apply to work and life today? Most of us would clearly say no. Beyond merely considering the number of hours worked, and recognizing work as taking substantially more than eight hours per day, the additional lens is the manner in which our daily 24 hours unfolds. Long gone are the days during which labour, recreation, and rest would proceed in a serial fashion.

Though we may have moved significantly from the origins of the working day, many of the same challenges that existed at the dawn of the First Industrial Revolution are in play today, and will likely become more acute in the near future. The topic of work-life balance has been of particular interest, with the work-life *integration* term receiving attention. In a nutshell, employees have more flexibility in their workday, being able to leave at 4pm to watch their children's school play, but can expect work demands to come out of the normal work hours also. Ruth Whippman on the The Pool blog [1] offered a refreshing, slightly cynical view:

> "Somehow, all the 'integrating' only ever seems to flow in one direction... taking time off in the middle of the workday for a kid's concert or a haircut never quite materializes. Instead, we answer emails crouching behind a bush, playing hide and seek with a four-year-old."

This is why a Chief Wellbeing Officer is required to help navigate through an increasingly complex working environment, so that potentially valuable ideas like work-life integration don't simply mean more work and less balance.

So what do *you* do every day?

So what about you? Have you reflected on your own work-life balance or integration? How do you spend the minutes and hours of your day? The following exercise is a worthwhile initial reflection.

Table 8.1. What is work anyway?

'Work' activity	Daily TIME spent on activity (Hours, minutes OR high-medium-low)	WHERE does it take place? (Office, park, home, commuting, long-haul travel, in the shower, etc.)
Meetings		
Reading		
Writing		
Thinking		
Planning		
Emails		
Anything else?		

We often use this exercise in the context of the MOVE element of the Sustaining Executive Performance (SEP) programme, highlighting that quality work need not be confined to the sedentary office time that characterizes most workplaces, and which compromises both health and performance. AOL chief executive Tim Armstrong considered the key metric for his executives as '10% thinking time'. They had to formally commit to 10% of their weekly time as being dedicated to thinking. How much time do you spend thinking through tough problems? How much time are you spending on other, perhaps less value-added, activities?

A common takeaway from the above exercise is that people discover their best thinking occurs in places other than the office. We conclude that leaving the office to take a shower when confronted with a tough problem may be taking things a little far, but stress the importance of moving and giving ourselves permission that work, especially quality work, need not be sedentary office time.

Figure 8.2. Scenario storyboard for a typical busy professional

And how does this way of working manifest itself throughout the day? Based on our design-thinking experience, we ask people to map out their typical day on the template below. We stress the importance of noting the small actions, which they may feel incidental, but which can have large ramifications. How they spend the first minutes of their day, for example, or their last, can impact heavily on their productivity and wellbeing that morning or the quality of their sleep, respectively. How they move between the main locations of their day, and the time spent at the office and home. The timing of meals and of course the quantity of work, rest, and play. The level of balance or integration becomes clear, and though many may have lived such a reality for years, it is interesting to note how impactful it can be for them – with a common takeaway being that they have no time for themselves – when it is on the paper in front of them. Having it on paper tends to make it more real.

Figure 8.3. Your typical working day. Try it!

"I don't have time!" is a frequent refrain in a modern-day professional life. Yet a reflection such as this will help you identify if you are spending the time you do have wisely. Perhaps change will include cutting away the unimportant tasks, delegating others, or simply finding a new time to do things so as to be more efficient. We have yet to find a case in our coaching work where a close look at the 168 hours available in a week does not offer the space to live a productive professional life that optimizes wellbeing. American author Laura Vanderkam tested her own limits as a working mother of four children in the *New York Times* article 'The Busy Person's Lies'. She logged over 17,000 half-hour blocks in a full year to analyse exactly how she was spending her time, finding that she was indeed busy, but that there was plenty of space also. She concluded there is no contradiction between a full life that also has space.

Your perfect productive day

Publications including *Fast Company* and *BBC Future* have looked at the topic of optimizing one's day in recent years, including the timing of different activities. Social media is awash with productivity info-graphics and other list-laden clickbait articles, yet some of the better tips include:

1. Try free writing immediately upon waking for best creativity (before your inner critic fully wakens up).

2. Drink coffee a couple of hours after waking instead of straight away (we are naturally alert after waking, given the body's release of cortisol which then dips a couple of hours later).

3. Do the hardest task of the day first when your energy and attention should be high.

4. Check emails in batches throughout the day, instead of being responsive to emails as you receive them.

5. Maximize the chances of your email being read by sending it between 10am and midday on weekdays.

6. Get away from your (uncluttered – keep it clean for better wellbeing) desk for lunch.

7. Call a loved one in the afternoon as an effective way of boosting your energy and mood.

8. Set priorities for the following day on the afternoon or evening before.

It is hard to argue for the universality of all of the above, yet many are worthy of experimentation. Our coaching work includes the consideration of these and others within a process that includes personal reflection, and time and energy audits.

The circadian rhythm

A human-based view of work needs to consider our biology, especially if considering energy. Productivity is reflective of a machine-based view of the world, but we are not machines, and the circadian rhythm (the biological process at play each day of our lives) offers valuable lessons for optimum health, wellbeing, and performance.

Figure 8.4. Thinking about our daily rhythms

The origins of circadian rhythm science can be traced to the fields of chronobiology and chronobiochemistry. In particular, the German botanists who formed a leading school of thought in these areas in the early 20th century. The rhythms that were so evident in nature, dating back to concepts such as the Linnaeus flower clock from 1751, provided inspiration for looking at those same rhythms in ourselves, with much of that focus taking place in the medical field to tackle disease – including cancer.

LINNAEUS
FLOWER CLOCK,
CARL LINNAEUS (1707-1780)

6am Spotted Cat's Ear opens

7am African Marigold opens

8am Mouse Ear Hawkweed opens

9am Prickly Sowthistle closes

10am Common Nipple Wort closes

11am Star of Bethlehem opens

12pm Passion Flower opens

1pm Childing Pink closes

2pm Scarlet Pimpernel closes

3pm Hawkbit closes

4pm Small Bindweed closes

5pm White Water Lily closes

6pm Evening Primrose opens

We find it fascinating and illuminating to uncover the work of such pioneers so far in advance of today's world of big data and the quantified self. Chronobiology, according to Professor Hugh Simpson is "the science of quantifying and investigating mechanisms of biological time structure, including the rhythmic manifestations of life".[2] Rhythms with different frequencies are found at all levels of the biological system, from the ecosystem, group, and individual to even the organ, tissue, cell, and sub-cellular levels. Such patterns are critical to the survival of the matter in question, and some of these manifestations on a human level are surprising:

1. We are taller in the morning than in the evening (up to 2cm). Over the course of a day our cartilage compresses, mostly within our spinal column, as a result of our physical actions. Sleep allows everything to relax and fully decompress.

2. We are physically stronger later in the day. Most athletics world records are broken in the afternoon or evening, when body temperature is highest, blood pressure is lowest, and lung function is more efficient.

3. Our core temperature varies during the day, dipping towards bedtime. Taking a hot shower or bath before bed can aid sleep, and researchers believe that the natural dip in temperature when we get out provides an additional signal to the brain that it is time to go to sleep. Our lowest temperature occurs around 5am – does pulling the covers over in those pre-dawn hours sound familiar?

In all cases, our connection with the natural environment is key, with the energy and cycles of the sun dictating our own daily pattern – principally that we are awake during the day when the sun is shining, and asleep at night when the sun has set. Though fluctuating height, strength, and temperature may not have much of a direct impact on work and wellbeing, other daily patterns do, including mood and energy. For example, doctors have long been aware of the link between sleep, sunlight, and mood, with research showing earlier discharge of hospitalized bipolar patients who were assigned to rooms with views of the east – presumably because the early morning light had an antidepressant effect. Research published in *Science,* which analysed 509 million tweets, found users more likely to tweet upbeat, enthusiastic messages between 6am and 9am.[3] Having our circadian rhythms out of balance can have a variety of physiological and psychological effects. Research has shown long-term night-shift workers to have a series of health issues, including obesity, cardiovascular disease, diabetes, and metabolic syndrome. The most common experience of this for many of us, certainly for the well-travelled business person, is jet-lag – essentially displacing our principal light-and-dark cycle. Physical tiredness and a lack of mental clarity may compromise performance and wellbeing, with cases even being found of severe depression. Many of the symptoms of jetlag are being replicated in our daily lives. Spending an excessive amount of time indoors without sufficient natural light during the day, followed by shining an excessive amount of digital devices into our heads at night, results in a constant 'social jetlag'. The pineal gland, positioned between our eyes, secretes melatonin, the hormone necessary for healthy sleep towards bedtime (normally starting around 9pm) with the fading of the day. Shining light into the pineal gland at night can suppress the production of that melatonin.

Resetting our natural rhythm, and therefore improving wellbeing and the many benefits that result, doesn't take long. Researchers from the University of Colorado found that a weekend of camping outdoors with no exposure to artificial light, reset the circadian rhythm, allowing the subjects to follow better sleep cycles on their return home.[4]

Many may be aware of the main energy fluctuations during a day as a result of our circadian rhythm; the siesta or nap zone in the mid-afternoon is now taken seriously at some leading companies who have installed nap-pods and rooms. The need to nap is not actually due to a large lunch (although it certainly can be compounded by one), but due to the fact that 3pm and 3am are the lowest energy points of our day. It's no coincidence that most suicides occur just after 3am. Being aware of our higher energy states is just as important. How do you spend the pockets of time between 10am and midday, and 4pm and 6pm when we are at our most alert? Most business cultures and individual habits result in email and heavy administrative work taking up the first peak period and a home commute taking up the second. Try recording your own 'energy audit' over the course of a week. When do you feel most alert and when do you have your best ideas? Are you making the most of that time?

Research in different fields points to the impact of such daily fluctuations. On average, people are worse at processing new information, planning, and resisting distractions as the day progresses. Decision fatigue theory points to the lower quality of our decisions as the day advances, with good decisions also dependent on mealtimes and eating the right food. Have you ever had a 'hangry' child? What makes you think lack of food would have a different effect on an adult?

Ethics are also at the mercy of our biology. When energy is low, people are more likely to behave unethically with others, having a greater tendency to lie in the afternoon than in the evening. Researchers call this 'psychological depletion', reflecting our experience of being cognitively weaker as the day wears on.

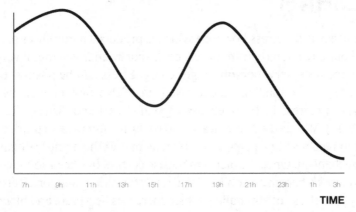

TIME

Figure 8.5. Fluctuating levels of alertness through the day

The best version of ourselves, as we have mentioned at several points in *Chief Wellbeing Officer*, is therefore a highly attainable concept that depends on daily biological variables as well as bigger-picture thinking, including purpose. Understanding our biochemistry and chronotype analysis allows us to fine-tune this endeavour.

Understanding our biochemistry

We believe ourselves to be rational beings, acting on the logic of any given situation, yet research such as psychological depletion, noted above, says otherwise. We are also at the mercy of our body's chemistry. Chemicals may rise and fall at different parts of the day in accordance with our circadian rhythm or as a result of different habitual actions, which helps to reinforce such habits. By understanding the processes at play we may better control such impulses when they arrive. The Stoic school of philosophy, which counted on high-profile proponents such as Roman Emperor Marcus Aurelius, often highlights how our impulses can derail our best intentions. An overview of the main chemicals in our working lives now follows.

Cortisol

Cortisol is the stress hormone which is produced naturally as part of our circadian rhythm. Levels peak shortly after waking, giving us the necessary 'oomph' to get going. Stress can be positive or negative – Canadian biochemist Hans Selye first defined two types of stress in 1936: eustress (good stress) and distress (bad stress). We need stress to learn and perform, and we also produce it in response to a perceived threat, as part of the 'fight-or-flight' mechanism. Once the alarm to release cortisol has been sounded, your body becomes mobilized and ready for action (supported also by the release of adrenaline, which increases heart rate and blood pressure). If there is no physical release of this fight-or-flight response – typical within a sedentary working environment, where threats are information-based and psychological – a build up of cortisol can cause a variety of physical and mental problems.

In our research we have found the benefits of simple coping mechanisms such as controlled diaphragmatic breathing. Fight-or-flight, the sympathetic part of our nervous system, characterizes many busy professionals who go through their days in a heightened state of arousal – responding to crises, eating poorly, taking stimulants, and being constantly online. We have used heart rate variability (HRV) analysis to show a return to the parasympathetic (or recovery) part of the nervous system.

Individual exercise to de-stress

If you feel that 'getting off the hamster wheel' is required, try the following. Lie flat on your back in a quiet room, bend your knees and keep your feet flat on the floor. Place both hands on your belly and breathe in through your nose to the count of six (use a timer like the MyCalmBeat app). Aim to raise your hands as high as possible through focusing that inhalation on your belly. Exhale to the count of six through your mouth, lowering your hands and belly once again. Repeat for three minutes, after which you will have moved from fight-or-flight mode to rest-and-digest, feeling more relaxed and in control.

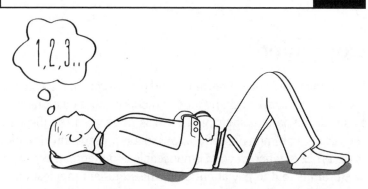

Figure 8.6. Controlled diaphragmatic breathing exercise

Serotonin

Serotonin is the wellbeing hormone and one of the key neurotransmitters – the chemical 'messengers' in our brain. It is responsible for the regulation of mood, aggression, appetite, and sleep. On an evolutionary level serotonin gave an organism good feelings towards its environment, and low levels of serotonin sparked dissatisfaction, urging the organism to relocate and/or change habits. Low serotonin levels result in increased appetite and vice versa. Depression, which is often caused by low serotonin levels, may lead to augmented food consumption, while exposure to light can increase serotonin.

Stanford marketing professor Baba Shiv highlights the importance of serotonin in decision-making, creativity, and leadership.[5] He values its role in providing a calm, relaxed state, as well as minimizing the negative effects of stress, believing it to support an opportunity-centric Type II mindset (as opposed to a Type I mindset that focuses on risk and failure). He highlights the decrease of serotonin throughout the day and also when we reach the age of 50, advising that organizations should design teams to include different ages in order to balance this. His principal recommendations come in the areas of exercise, diet, and sleep, which we covered in chapter six.

Dopamine

Dopamine is the reward hormone and plays a role in many forms of addiction, from drugs and food to modern-day addictions such as social media and smartphones. It is more than the pleasure chemical, a common misconception, as it represents the first part in the process, where reward is noticeable or better than expected. The brain is told to pay attention to the stimulant in question as it may be important for survival in the future, prioritizing it over older, more predictable rewards. Many researchers believe it is more about drug wanting than liking. The anticipation and unpredictability of the drug in question – say social media use through red bubble notifications – is therefore *the main reason for persistent use in spite of negative consequences*. The negative consequences of heroin or alcohol are of course well known, with greater understanding beginning to emerge on digital device addiction – compromised wellbeing being the main result. Social media designers play on the brain function associated with dopamine, with features such as notifications appearing after a short delay (likened by some as playing a slot machine) in order to maximize the brain's anticipation and levels of dopamine.

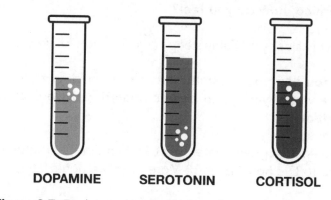

DOPAMINE   **SEROTONIN**   **CORTISOL**

Figure 8.7. Find your chemical balance[6]

Chronotype analysis

The chemical responses of our habits therefore personalize our circadian rhythm, with our individual chronotype adding to that personalisation. We either have a natural propensity to rise early in the day, meaning we prefer to go to sleep early (termed 'lark') or rise later, with the corresponding later time to go to bed (termed 'owl'). The natural population distribution applies, so many of us will be neither a lark or an owl.

ARE YOU A **LARK,** AN **OWL,** OR **NEITHER?**

(Adapted from the Morningness-Eveningness Questionnaire MEQ)

4 **1. How's your appetite in the first half hour after you wake up in the morning?**

(a) Very poor (b) Fairly poor (c) Fairly good (d) Very good

3 **2. For the first half hour after you wake up in the morning, how do you feel?**

(a) Very sleepy (b) Fairly sleepy (c) Fairly alert (d) Very alert

3 **3. You have no commitments the next day; at what time would you go to bed compared with your usual bedtime?**

(a) Seldom or never later (b) Less than one hour later (c) One to two hours later (d) More than two hours later

2 **4. You are going to get fit. A friend suggests joining their fitness class between 7am and 8am. How do you think you'd perform?**

(a) Would be on good form (b) Would be on reasonable form (c) Would find it difficult (d) Would find it very difficult

3 **5. At what time do you feel sleepy and need to go to bed?**

(a) 8-9pm (b) 9-10.15pm (c) 10.15pm-12.45am (d) 12.45-2am (e) 2-3am

6. If you went to bed at 11pm, how sleepy would you be?

(a) Not at all sleepy (b) A little sleepy (c) Fairly sleepy (d) Very sleepy

7. One night you have to remain awake between 4am and 6am. You have no commitments the next day. Which suits you best?

(a) Not go to bed until 6am (b) Nap before 4am and nap after 6am (c) Sleep before 4am and nap after 6am (d) Sleep before 4am and remain awake after 6am

8. Suppose you can choose your own work hours, but have to work five hours in the day. When would you like to start work?

(a) Between midnight and 5am (b) 3-8am (c) 8-10am (d) 10am-2pm (e) 2-4pm (e) 4pm-midnight

9. At what time of day do you feel your best?

(a) Midnight-5am (b) 5am-9am (c) 9am-11am (d) 11am-5pm (e) 5pm-10pm (f) 10pm-midnight

10. Do you think of yourself as a morning or evening person?

(a) Morning type (b) More morning than evening (c) More evening than morning (d) Evening type

QUESTION SCORES

1. (a) [1] (b) [2] (c) [3] (d) [4]
2. (a) [1] (b) [2] (c) [3] (d) [4]
3. (a) [4] (b) [3] (c) [2] (d) [1]
4. (a) [4] (b) [3] (c) [2] (d) [1]
5. (a) [5] (b) [4] (c) [3] (d) [2] (e) [1]
6. (a) [0] (b) [2] (c) [3] (d) [5]
7. (a) [1] (b) [2] (c) [3] (d) [4]
8. (a) [1] (b) [5] (c) [4] (d) [3] (e) [2] (e) [1]
9. (a) [1] (b) [5] (c) [4] (d) [3] (e) [2] (f) [1]
10. (a) [6] (b) [4] (c) [2] (d) [0]

SCORING

8-12: Strong owl
13-20: Moderate owl

34-41: Moderate lark
42-46: Strong lark

21-33: Neither owl nor lark

So what did you get?

Strong or moderate owl

Owls have the hardest time fitting into the business and wider social convention of starting work early in the morning and getting to bed at a time that allows them to rise early, which is much easier for larks. For natural owls, gaining the maximum amount of sunlight (getting outside, even on a cloudy day, still makes a significant difference) during the first half of the day will help to ensure your natural 'clock' begins to wind down a little sooner each day.

Strong or moderate lark

Larks may experience difficulties coping with late-night activities such as business dinners, parties, or late-night deadlines. The same hack holds as for owls but in reverse – aim to stay indoors during the first half of the day and gain as much outdoor light exposure during the afternoon to improve alertness toward the second half of the day.

Neither owl nor lark

You could be right down the middle (most of us will be) or this could be the result of conditioning over many years of following the same schedule, even if this is non-optimal for you. Take an experimental approach; try and get a little more natural daylight during the day and take care with light at night. See what happens.

Paying greater attention to your natural light and dark cycles has many benefits for health, wellbeing, and performance, improved sleep being chief among them, with other research pointing to benefits for weight management. Artificial light does not give us the necessary effects, reaching an average of around 5,000 lux in the brightest office environment, with outdoor natural light in the region of 100,000 lux.

Understanding your own chronotype is useful, with value also in being able to empathize with other people. We have coached many executives who have a strong preference for one type, yet assuming the rest of their team has the same profile leads to inefficient meetings and poorly managed expectations. It is better to hold those key meetings when everyone is performing at their best. Think also about your home environment. Finding it difficult to have that important conversation with your partner early in the morning or late at night? Your chronotypes may be vastly different!

When does your team get their best ideas? Highest energy? A lark working a late schedule or an owl working an early schedule is a chronotype mismatch that can be problematic. Leaders should understand that employees are not being lazy or disinterested in the work, simply that their biology doesn't support their working patterns.

Society tends to regard larks as hard-working conscientious types and owls as slightly work-shy mavericks. Such beliefs are a result of the societal structures we have built around the typical working day, which may be less prevalent as we move further into the Fourth Industrial Revolution. Though a 24-7-hour society is not in everyone's interests for optimal wellbeing, the 9-5 working pattern is surely loosening. By providing the right structure and designing the right teams – for example, by choosing people who are near their circadian peak at times in the day when you want that team to perform – we may impact greatly on business value and the wellbeing of individuals, since they will be well-matched to their working environment.

Jim Rohn, regarded my many as the pioneer of self-help management said that, "either you run the day or the day runs you". Regardless of what you want from the day in question, understanding the main biological patterns will allow greater balance, productivity, and wellbeing, for you and your teams. We are all governed by such rhythms, yet are unique at the same time. We call this 'circadian diagnostics' and see it as a crucial step in fulfilling the vision of Chief Wellbeing Officer. Though the Spanish Government has started a consultation on the country's timezone it could be that the political issues of late 2017 will again mean it is forgotten. Yet the awarding of the 2017 Nobel Prize in Physiology or Medicine for research on the circadian rhythm shows its great importance for our modern world. It is an area we believe will become even more significant as we move further into the Fourth Industrial Revolution.

PART 3

OFFICER

The third and final part of

Chief Wellbeing Officer focuses

on the HOW of action. We do not

presume to know all the answers

but hope to inspire you to act by

highlighting the right questions

9
DESIGN FOR WELLBEING

"There is an order to things. That's what we do here. We keep order."

Lieutenant Joshi, *Bladerunner 2049*

BARCELONA is a vibrant city of design. From the historical figures and movements we have covered so far in other parts of the book, including Gaudí and Picasso, to the design education of today in leading schools that teach fashion, engineering, and architecture, the creative story of the city is one of its undoubted features. And that story includes a significant link to the most famous design school of all. Ludwig Mies van der Rohe directed the Bauhaus from 1930 to 1933, when it was shut down by its own leadership under pressure from the Nazi Party. Part of his ascent to the directorship of this pioneering centre that integrated art, craft, and technology must be attributed to his design of the Barcelona Pavilion, which he built for the German section of the 1929 International Exposition. This modernist marvel was designed to be "an ideal zone of tranquillity" for the weary traveller as they made their way through the sections of a busy international fair, with the driving rationale of wellbeing evident also in the creation of the famous Barcelona Chair, which van der Rohe created for the King and Queen of Spain to sit on and rest during their visit.

This is the first chapter in the third and final part of *Chief Wellbeing Officer*. Officer focuses on the *how*, providing instruction on moving to action. Design for Wellbeing opens this final direction in our narrative through a consideration of design as a means of doing. Here, we take a broad view of the skillset that supports any officer as they build and sustain a more human-based high-performing culture at work. This discussion will set the foundation for the following chapters, which show a more specific application of design; in the next chapter we present a behaviour-change framework for designing new habits and routines, with chapter 11 detailing how we can design our environment.

Furthermore, the skills focus of this chapter builds on an understanding of our human biology in chapter eight and links to the habits focus of chapter ten to give us the ABC of design for wellbeing:

- **A: Attitude** represents the senior leadership skills that can be borrowed from design-thinking to create a more human workplace. There is great value in integrating more exposure to ambiguity, observation, iteration, and empathy in daily leadership practice.

- **B: Behaviour** concerns the discrete behaviours that make up the daily work of the workforce at large and our understanding of how these habits may be changed. Connecting these behaviours to culture is of increasing interest to companies around the world.

- **C: Chronobiology** looks at the natural biological rhythms that make up our daily lives. In an age where work is potentially, and increasingly, 24-7, recognizing that we are not machines and subject to our human biology is critical. The vast exposure given to sleep in recent years is, we believe, the first example of many where our circadian rhythm will feature more prominently as a business concern.

What is design?

Design is the process whereby something is created. This creative process is followed by some manufacture or elaboration, so that the design becomes reality. Design is therefore about *doing*, quite ironic given the standard worldwide acceptance of the design-thinking term. Design cannot be passively learned, and so some practice in designing, through a mixture of sketching, prototyping, observing, or interviewing, is necessary to learn. Although there is freedom within a necessarily creative endeavour, structure and rigour are required for design to work, and to produce the desired end result.

Design begins with an objective, sometimes a formalized brief, and follows a creative process, whereby potential solutions or concepts are generated and then evaluated, before the necessary details are elaborated to move that design towards reality. Though many different models of the design process exist, all follow the same general dynamic, moving through cycles of abstraction and concreteness. The solution 'space' of the design will expand and contract, following a flow of divergence and convergence, from the early stages of understanding the user and/or problem, to generating concepts and prototypes that fulfill those needs, before detailing the concept that best fulfills those needs. Several iterations of the process may also take place, which allows thorough evaluation of the designed solution by sharing it with the end user.

Here we take a broad view of the skillset that supports any officer as they build and sustain a more human-based high-performing culture at work.

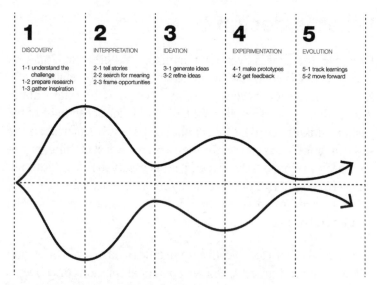

Figure 9.1. The IDEO design-thinking process

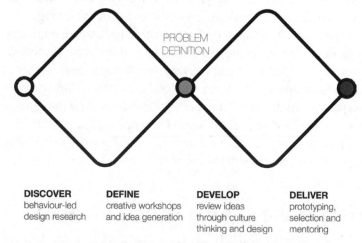

Figure 9.2. The UK Design Council 'Double Diamond'

As well as being a process-driven concept, design contains, at its core, certain characteristics that allow us to apply the value of design to different fields, beyond its traditional product and engineering origins. These include:

- **Human:** Above all things, design is human. It looks to create a world that satisfies the needs we have as human beings. In our emerging always-on machine-driven world, design will play an increasingly key role in maintaining the human element. Human needs, within the context of Chief Wellbeing Officer, regard a workplace and corresponding culture that supports health, wellbeing, and sustainable performance. Needs change, in line with the changing experience of the employee, say during a business quarter, financial year, or even career. These needs may also exist on an extreme level – of particular interest in design, because these extreme needs are often characteristic of lead users, a part of the population who may offer insight into the future because they experience such needs ahead of the general population.

- **Hidden:** Such needs may be difficult to articulate, and designers question aspects of our human life that are often difficult to see or appreciate as being necessary to improve. Former MIT professor and frequently cited source in the design field Donald Schön said that "we know more than we can say", and the subconscious part of our brains often drive our actions. Gerald Zaltman, a Harvard professor, has stated that conscious activity represents only 5% of cognition. The hidden 95% is therefore the target of design if we want to satisfy human needs. The 'deep-dive' is a common term in any design-focused effort that relates to this phenomena, and is represented in figure 9.3.

- **Methods:** Design is equipped through various tools or methods employed at different stages of the process to progress towards an optimum solution. They may be used to understand the user, challenge assumptions, generate concepts, and essentially connect the need, user, and designer. Many of these methods have been taken from other fields including anthropology and engineering, which also highlights the diversity in design. Design teams are almost always multidisciplinary and may contain engineers, MBAs, lawyers, and doctors, who pursue a broad, exploratory approach. Although such teamwork may advance within the workplace, methods are designed to enable their implementation in the real context or environment of the user, commonly referred to as the 'field'.

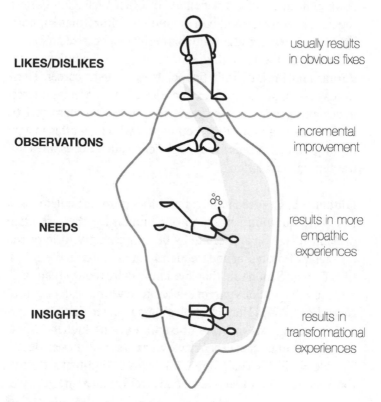

Figure 9.3. The design-driven deep-dive

Design for X

One of the most practical approaches to design is Design for X, which comes from the engineering or product design field. X denotes the area of focus to be optimised within the development of the product, such as environment, usability, or manufacturability.

Our intention in *Chief Wellbeing Officer* is to develop a type of design for a wellbeing framework that can be used in an organization.

The general best practice of design is therefore fine-tuned to the specific needs of the endeavour in question.

Much of the popularity of design in recent years is due to its universality, and power to tackle a broad range of problems in different fields. Many of these applications could be designated *wicked* problems – complex issues, often within the social sphere and developing world that require a fresh look. IDEO published the HCD (human-centered design) toolkit in 2009, with the specific intention of overcoming challenges in the nonprofit world through a deep understanding of human needs. Partly funded by the Bill & Melinda Gates Foundation, the toolkit is a free innovation guide designed specifically for NGOs and social enterprises that work with impoverished communities in Africa, Asia, and Latin America. Innovations have resulted in the areas of clean drinking water, blood donation, and heart defibrillation.

Our intention in *Chief Wellbeing Officer* is to develop a type of design for a wellbeing framework that can be used in an organization. This will help our main aim of moving health and wellbeing to a more senior level in an organization. Having the right tools and methods, something that the design field is so good at doing, will allow a strategic approach to a complex issue. Much of the content presented so far in the book is part of this emergent framework.

Given the different ways and contexts in which we can view well-being, the Design for Wellbeing term already exists but we feel that guidance to help drive health, wellbeing, and performance at a sufficiently senior level of the organization is lacking. Nevertheless, we can take inspiration from the many other approaches that already exist.

The Glasgow School of Art is one of the top-ten art schools in the world. At its new creative campus in Forres in the north of Scotland it looks at how design may improve innovation in different areas of business and society. The Scottish Highlands base provides a set of unique challenges around geographical distribution that may help inspire different innovations that can be applied within traditional urban centres. For example, in the healthcare setting, if a patient requires over two hours' travel time to get to a hospital, how may the experience be re-designed? And is there any value from this re-imagination that can be applied to traditional settings? 'Innovation from the edge' is their term, which links to some of our previous comments on taking a fresh look at wicked problems, and may also share some characteristics with other design-driven approaches such as reverse innovation, in which solutions conceived in the developing world are implemented in the developed world, given their consideration of certain extreme needs.

Wellbeing is one of the main themes at the campus driven by the Digital Health Institution, which works with the National Health Service in Scotland and the Scottish Government in the design of public services. Experience labs bring together clinicians, patients, and technology providers to co-create services that better cope with an ageing population. Designing preferable futures is the vision, and wellbeing is at the heart of that. Greater societal wellbeing, as we showed in chapter four, is being targeted around the world and a more senior consideration of wellbeing in business will help.

Design skills for the Chief Wellbeing Officer

As noted above, the best way of understanding design and de-sign-thinking is through doing. This practice may come in the form of using the tools, methods, and processes of a designer in tackling a problem, while we can also integrate the skillset of a designer within our leadership practice. The first, more conventional application of design, creates new value through a newly designed product, service, or experience, yet we need to protect the value we already have through our daily leadership practice. There are several highly valuable and transferable design skills that can improve this daily practice. Maybe you already practice some of them; we do not brand these as being exclusively from the design field. Indeed, the increasing popularity and use of design in the past few years has been due in large part to its ability to combine different approaches from a wide variety of fields and bring them together in a usable whole.

Being a design thinker doesn't mean you are a designer. Some designers are not good design thinkers. But by being a better design thinker, we believe you can be a better leader and a true Chief Wellbeing Officer, regardless of your specific role and responsibilities. Whether you possess a formal title in HR that has board presence and influence, are a family member who looks at the lives and wellbeing of all the family, a sports coach or volunteer in the local community, or a fresh graduate in an organization, large or small, the following design-based skillset will help create value. Since we believe that design cannot be passively learned, we frame the following skills in terms of gaining more practice.

By being a better design thinker, we believe you can be a better leader and a true Chief Wellbeing Officer.

Practice more exposure to ambiguity

Experienced design thinkers are comfortable with ambiguity. And in today's complex professional life, ambiguity is an increasing feature. Today's executive life is a complicated affair where the boundaries between work, rest, and play are blurred. Much has been written on the VUCA reality of business and society today, where volatility, uncertainty, complexity and ambiguity are increasingly present elements. Bob Johansen of the Institute for the Future proposed the VUCA Prime framework as a leadership response to this environment. V is for 'vision' which is required to navigate a volatile business context, U stands for 'understanding' to make sense of volatility and communicate effectively, C for 'clarity' to set the foundation for action, and A for 'agility' in order to move quickly and effectively.

A manager may have experience in the cognitive dissonance of ambiguity through their dealings with opposing views in business. Whether it be operations and innovation or short-term versus long-term results, senior leaders have long been aware of the need to build an ambidextrous organization that has to look both ways at once in order to thrive. The F. Scott Fitzgerald quote seems to fit well here: "The test of a first-rate intelligence is the ability to hold two opposed ideas in mind at the same time and still retain the ability to function."

Exposing both our professional and personal lives to more ambiguity, though uncomfortable in the short-term, may help to uncover new practices and habits that drive superior health, wellbeing, and performance. The next time you're ready to action one of your long-held beliefs or values, consider first the exact opposite view. Although you may not follow this opposite view, which may be perceived as a lack of authenticity by your colleagues, it at least opens up a whole range of possibilities and options that may never have been considered before. There is much to be said for *being comfortable with being uncomfortable* in today's rapidly changing environment.

The next time you're ready to action one of your long-held beliefs or values, consider first the exact opposite view.

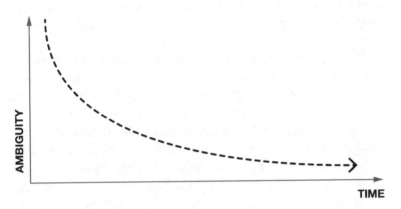

Figure 9.4. The ambiguity curve

Stanford-based educators William Cockayne and Tamara Carleton highlight the high level of ambiguity at the beginning of the design process.[1] This is part of the reason why designers are comfortable with ambiguity – since they trust in the process. Fully embracing ambiguity allows new and innovative solutions to be considered, and full immersion is possible since there is confidence in it being a temporary state. It is more like an opportunity to be embraced while the window remains open, rather than an inconvenience to be endured.

Practice more empathy

In design we ask: how may we fully understand the needs of another human being if we have not walked in their shoes? For increased engagement in the organization, leaders need to manage in a more empathetic manner. At the end of the day, work is still work. Employees must maintain professionalism and understand their responsibilities, yet the employer has to take their duty of care seriously. And this duty of care must encompass the whole picture, including home and family life, as well as notions of health and wellbeing. Such *liberal paternalism* allows diagnosis and preventative action before full-blown crises occur, including the best talent walking out the door. As we discussed in chapter five, empathy is a key part of developing emotional intelligence.

Running in the hamster wheel of daily corporate life can dehumanize the best of us. Taking a more holistic view of management to pay attention to the small signals coming from the teams we lead can include more notions of personal care. As a leader, are you paying attention to the signals from your team and able to hold an empathetic conversation? Important signals could include excessive weekend email communication, skipping lunch at one's desk, or a continual disregard of the importance of sleep. Acting on these may help create high-performing teams as well as help fulfill an organization's duty of care.

Listening skills are an important part of an empathetic conversation. Start with a commitment to talk less! More talking and less listening tends to happen with more seniority. If the balance isn't maintained there is little value in that conversation other than instructing or lecturing. Leadership is not the same as management. Adopting a coaching mindset can therefore be of value, which includes listening without judging or offering solutions. May we also apply empathy inwards? We often coach executives to be more kind to *themselves* and understand that work doesn't only need to be about suffering.

A final consideration regards lead or extreme users, a well-established design technique where we examine the needs of those who exist at an extreme point of some scale. Once examined, this can offer clues to resolving the similar needs of those with a less severe nature. Extreme users in a work environment may include young parents (struggling, say, with sleep deprivation or feeling overwhelmed) or those suffering from depression or bereavement. Does the physical and social environment of the organization offer a supporting culture for these people and the workforce at large?

Practice more iteration

Iteration concerns the repeating element of a process. In design, the iterative loop (traditionally covering problem definition, gaining empathy, concept generation, and validation) helps to accelerate progress in comparison to one long linear process, where there is less insight into the impact of your decisions, or, more specifically, the cause and effect.

Iterating towards a solution isn't an easy proposition for today's manager. Dealing with the healthy critique and criticism of a well-formed yet individually developed idea can leave many managers uneasy, yet the collaborative, iterated solution that builds on the initial idea will be far superior. We often hold on to the 'straw man' solution – and feel an emotional connection to the first fully formed idea or concept we produce, yet for the best ideas and value this should merely be regarded as the prototype, a primer for discussion that could, and should, be ripped apart. How can you simulate, experiment, or prototype more in your normal work rather than always trying to get it right first time?

For iteration in leadership practice, we highlight two main features: speed and experimentation. A faster speed is possible since we will conduct the same or similar steps again, and be able to adapt or improve the first approximation. A leadership example comes from Telefónica CEO Jose María Álvarez-Pallete when describing his approach to decision-making:[2]

> "I think that taking decisions quickly is important. The balance between execution, agility, and a good logical reflection is important. But, you know, I rather do it quickly and then try to adapt, than to delay things. Because delaying things has a multiplying effect on the organization."

What are your own principal processes? These could be your own personal approaches to leadership and management activity including decision-making, or more organizational processes. What is the typical cycle time for those processes? One month? One year? Can you shorten it? Reduce it by half?

The reduced cycle time of a process allows us to view the second main feature of iteration: experimentation. Trying out new ways of doing things on a first pass helps to accelerate learning and ensures sustainable success. Lego has successfully reinvented itself over the past ten years, moving from a position of near bankruptcy to becoming a globally recognized innovation leader. The company CEO Jørgen Vig Knudstorp said that: "Every year we throw out the trophies and start again." Starting again may be more to do with attitude and mindset than the actual operational details of company processes, yet there is no doubt that such a mindset will encourage experimentation and a continual refresh of the way of working.

Yet experimentation needs to be carried out under the right conditions. One of the probable outcomes of experimentation is failure. A key reflection is to identify what represents a non-critical context, where failure can be exploited as a learning opportunity rather than a catastrophe. Experimentation should not be employed therefore when the stakes are high, dealing with a new client or reporting quarter-end results.

Athletes know how to try different things in the off-season during training, or even competition that is not perceived as the main objective. For example, six-time Olympic track-cycling champion Chris Hoy employed different tactics in races during non-Olympic years. Falling off the bike or failure was a painful consequence of some of these experiments, yet at the Olympic Games, by far the most important focus of a track-cyclist's career, tried-and-tested strategies were the order of the day, often as a result of the valuable experimentation and failure that occurred between the Olympic cycle. Failure helps in the learning process, as long as failure doesn't occur in a mission-critical context. How can you create the 'safe spaces' that allow people to experiment, fail, and try something for the first time?

The adaptive leadership methodology[3] advocates smart experimentation by targeting small initiatives that are perhaps under the radar or non-core activities. Such tweaking allows a view of the cause and effect of certain changes without causing significant disruption. Figure 9.5 below shows the importance of changing only a manageable amount of existing operations and experimenting with new ways of working before finally aligning with the statu quo.

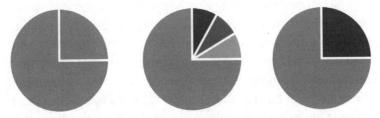

Figure 9.5. Running smart experiments according to adaptive leadership principles

A final view of iteration for leadership links to 'getting on the balcony' – the value of gaining distance from a situation. Some level of intervention is then required in order to fully test if those observations are correct, before repeating the cycle.

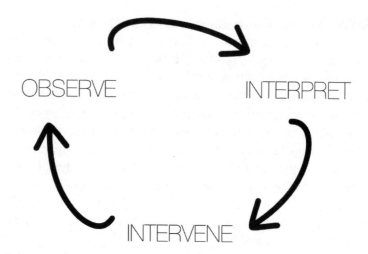

Figure 9.6. The iterative intervention cycle

We have practiced this in something called the triangle exercise. A class group is first randomly distributed in a large area such as a sports field. Each person is then asked to form an invisible triangle with two other people (without letting those people know they are picking them). Then the whole group moves, first in a clockwise direction for a few minutes, then anti-clockwise. Given that everybody has formed their triangle with two other people, we soon see a contrasting mix of people walking slow, fast, and even running in different directions to maintain their triangle. Observers from a vantage point high above the pitch can see patterns emerge and the source of harmony and chaos, but are powerless to intervene. Those on the pitch may affect quite a rapid change in the overall dynamic but as they are only concentrating on their group, they fail to see the big picture.

Iterating through the observe-interpret-intervene cycle may take place over a period of months in a consulting project or years in academic research, yet leadership activity often calls for much shorter timeframes, even counted in seconds.

Practice more observation

Getting on the balcony leads us to consider deep observation – another key skill of a design thinker. Observation does not happen in isolation and often serves as the precursor to asking powerful questions. For example, in ethnographic field research (which forms many of the initial stages of design research projects), observing real users in their natural environment will often be combined with asking those same people why they carry out a specific action, or how they're feeling in that moment.

Employing a designer's eye allows us to reflect on the rationale of why something exists – its use or function – and also helps in observing a commonly-seen view or object as if for the first time. As well as applying to physical objects, such an approach may be employed for experiences. Observing the dynamics at play in a meeting or office environment may help a deeper understanding of what transpires. We may therefore help surface and challenge assumptions around any issues in the workplace. Day-to-day business is characterized by a close-up view of many problems. With more years' experience we accumulate skills and knowledge, and operate to an extent on autopilot – a sign of competence. Yet by being more mindful of practice, many benefits can be generated for our own self-leadership and leadership of others.

Observation therefore drives a rich picture of the employee experience, which may be complemented by other means including feedback analysis, technology tracking, and data analytics. We have worked with our coaching clients in a similar fashion to redesign their professional day, which fits with many of the points raised in chapter eight. The following two examples show this approach.

CASE EXAMPLE 1

We worked with a banking executive on excessive fatigue experienced soon after a promotion. The first key change to the daily routine was the commute to work, for years unchanged as a 35-minute journey on a moped in heavy city traffic. With the increase in quality and quantity of decisions in the new role, we identified the issue of decision fatigue as being a key factor, with much of that precious decision-making energy being used on the stressful (though accustomed) morning commute. We replaced the moped journey with a scheduled daily private taxi, allowing the executive some free time, arriving at the office relaxed and with decision-making energy at optimum levels. With longer, more intense meetings also a characteristic of the new role we also instigated practice around deep belly breathing to bring calm and an even temperament, as leaving the room was often not an option.

CASE EXAMPLE 2

A group corporate learning director we worked with had a heavy travel schedule, logging high air and ground miles within demanding days where social engagements took just as much of a toll as core work. We focused on the ability to recover on the road, tailoring actions after conducting an analysis of her chronotype (the lark-owl questionnaire of the previous chapter). A personalized jetlag strategy was designed with specific actions, including a tailored routine for sleeping better on a plane and practice around being able to nap during long ground transfers.

As well as the working day, the employee experience may be traced on different levels, from varying timeframes – such as the business quarter, financial year, or even career – to discrete experiences such as training and onboarding.

Practicing more observation as an individual also greatly increases the personal wellbeing of the manager in question through increased exposure to silence and using the full range of our senses. Mindfulness practice is beneficial in part due to these reasons.

Practice more understanding

The previous elements of ambiguity, empathy, iteration and observation will lead to understanding, provided we pay attention to one more critical leadership characteristic: the 'hold'. As busy professionals we often rush to action, believing in the necessity of motion for results. Yet the value of the pause cannot be overstated. Reflecting deeply on information gained through practicing ambiguity, empathy, iteration, and observation will yield significant insight and opportunity.

Adaptive leadership encourages managers to hold back from rapid definition of a management task in the workplace so as to open up new and fresh possibilities. Diagnosing and reframing the problem ought to be the focus, instead of jumping to the solution. Defining the right question is often more difficult than finding the right answer.

We call these design skills the design vowels, the AEIOU of a more human language of leadership. Vowels are the main carriers of our voices; it is impossible to speak without them. We believe the design vowels will help to amplify your leadership. Design, though creative and flexible, essentially restores order. As the famed designer and educator Victor Papanek said: "Design is the conscious effort to impose meaningful order."

Design trades in *insights* – the deep-lying, non-obvious, yet often simple pieces of knowledge and understanding that drive

Know your **design vowels** to practice a more human-based language of leadership:

Ambiguity
Empathy
Iteration
Observation
Understanding

Defining the right question is often more difficult than finding the right answer.

next-generation innovations. By knowing and practicing the design vowels in daily leadership practice, managers will be able to drive the next-generation workplace, one that improves the engagement of the workforce at large through allowing wellbeing, and humanity, to flourish.

The Barcelona Pavilion sits discretely to this day near the original site of the 1929 International Exposition. Faithful to one of van der Rohe's guiding beliefs that less is more, we're sure he would also approve that it seems to be one of Barcelona's tourist secrets, far from the bustle of some of the other attractions in the city. Go there, stay a while in relative calm, and feel the full power of design wash over you and increase your wellbeing.

Figure 9.7. The Barcelona Pavilion

10

THE SEVEN HACKS OF HIGHLY EFFECTIVE HABITS

"Big things have small beginnings."

David, *Prometheus*

IF you want a hassle-free food-shopping experience *sans* queues while visiting Barcelona (outside of the hottest of tourist spots), go between 1.30pm and 3.30pm. The time traditionally reserved for siesta may not actually involve many naps these days but it's certainly not the time when Catalans go to the supermarket.

Clearly defined daily habits such as these surprised us both when we first came to live in Spain, in contrast to the UK and US, where patterns of movement in society are less clear. After living in Barcelona a number of years, one may pick up on certain other habits that allow an effective strategy to be put in place, depending on your needs. Feel like an atmosphere-rich breakfast? Go to the local café for a *café amb llet* at 10am. Want to go to the beach when people from Barcelona actually outnumber tourists? Head down at 4pm and stick around for an aperitif as you watch the sun going down. Feel like exploring further afield and the gorgeous Costa Brava north of the city? Just stay off the roads between 4-6pm on Fridays and 6-8pm on Sundays and you'll ensure an average speed above 5km/h.

Such knowledge of societal habits and cultural norms allows you to take the best bits of living in a city that can feel surprisingly intimate – even though it is populated by 1.6 million people and most of its square kilometres house more than 20,000 people.

Technology is increasingly being used to uncover such patterns and exploit the insights. In fact, 80% of data now has a location component – yet only 10% of it is used in decision-making. CARTO is a location-intelligence platform that allows the user to find tangible outcomes in their location data. For city planners, such information allows them to target advertising campaigns for exhibitions, provide additional public bus routes or even decide which languages to provide services in at certain tourism offices across the city. Florence Broderick, who works in solutions mar- keting at CARTO, shared her thoughts on the value of such data:

> "Before the era of the smartphone and IoT, we relied on surveys to understand citizen and tour- ist behaviour, asking small samples of people to declare their habits and preferences. Now we can understand a city's real-time pulse, observing behaviour in an anonymized and aggregated way to drive city decision-making – making the most of the fact 95% of people keep their smartphone with a one-metre reach 24 hours a day. Everything happens somewhere, and leading smart cities, such as Barcelona, are making location intelligence a cornerstone of their governance strategies for that reason."

Habits form culture

Identifying such well-defined behavioural patterns in the work-place may not be as easy. At least those that have the biggest potential to improve wellbeing and performance. For this rea-son, we believe it's important to look at the discrete, individual level of habits. By empowering people with a knowledge of how to either build new positive habits, or stop a more damaging one in its tracks, we may help build high-performing teams.

Habits in the workplace can have a significant impact on an organizational as well as individual level. Habits form routines and behaviour, which form culture when aggregated on a team level. PwC's Kristy Hull, writing in *Strategy+Business* in May 2017 notes how a critical few behaviours can help shape organizational culture. She highlights the importance of keystone behaviours, patterns of acting that are tangible, repeatable, observable, and measurable, and which have the potential to achieve a company's objectives. These are the critical few behaviours with good reason, as she believes people can really only remember and change three to five behaviours at one time. This is part of a wider effort being driven by Jon Katzenbach, one of the authors of the 1992 book, *The Wisdom of Teams*. He suggests that rather than tackling culture head-on, which can be a daunting task likely to end in failure, a company may have better success identifying and trying to change a select few behaviours that will positively influence culture once implemented across the organization.

Amazon provides a good example. At the company, no one speaks during the first ten to 30 minutes of a meeting, using that time instead to read in detail a printed memo from the meeting chair that they are seeing for the first time. The memo is not sent by email ahead of the meeting, which would result in a cursory glance by most, with the deep understanding and healthy critique of the content able to drive a participatory, value-added discussion. It is reflective of our notes on iteration as one of the design vowels in the previous chapter, allowing the company to move beyond the 'straw man' first solution towards a well-developed product that the company is increasingly known for.

Addressing habits may also help the alignment of an individual's values with that of their employer. Writing in *Inc* in July 2017, Adam Fridman highlighted factors that may help forge a stronger connection between the personal and organizational level, including several of the themes we have developed in this book, including purpose, happiness, and learning.

We believe habits to be a source of untapped potential for an organization. As human beings we like habits. They represent the known, give us control, and help us save energy and deal with stress. The esteemed 19th-century American psychologist, William James said that: "All our life, so far as it has definite form, is but a mass of habits – practical, emotional, and intellectual – systematically organized for our weal or woe, and bearing us irresistibly toward our destiny, whatever the latter may be."

In *The Seven Habits of Highly Effective People,* Stephen Covey invented the self-help management genre. The book, first published in 1989, has sold over 25 million copies worldwide. Knowing which habits are conducive to professional success and personal happiness continues to receive significant attention today, yet knowing how to make those habits stick is another matter. There is a wealth of potential insight in considering the subconscious part of our brains. Part of the appeal of design-thinking in recent years has been a powerful set of design methods that aim to shine light on the subconscious or hidden part of the user. For leadership practice, the design vowels of the previous chapter may help explore and understand workplace habits.

We process a large amount of automatic, subconscious activity every day but implementing new, positive habits, or breaking negative ones, is a significant challenge. Types of thinking and decision-making are natural areas of analysis in the working context. Though some of the studies may be questionable, a quick 'wisdom of Google' search puts our daily decisions at more than 30,000, with only 70 of those being conscious. Certainly, of more reliability is the work of Nobel Prize winner Daniel Kahneman, who writes on two systems of thinking.[1] Fast or System 1 thinking, which is the subconscious part of our brains and much more frequent; and slow or System 2, our conscious self which is much less frequent. It is clear that we need both. Without habits we'd be unlikely to proceed very far in our daily lives – if for example every single decision were to be slow and conscious. Yet stepping back from our normal routines and being wary of our competence and experience that results in automatic patterns is also healthy. More mindful practice may result in a higher degree of System 2 thought.

Although we may perceive certain behaviour as good or bad in others, it is not always so clear-cut for ourselves. When we create a habit the brain stops participating fully in the decision-making process, and doesn't distinguish between good and bad habits. So what are the tactics that help us take a step back, to first identify the good and bad behavioural patterns in our own lives and teams, and have a better chance of changing them?

We have developed the 7S model, comprised of seven behaviour 'hacks', a term of increasing usage the past few years which merits a brief presentation.

We see three elements to *hacking*. First, it is an iterative process. One long cycle of designing, implementing, and reflecting on the results of a new behaviour is unlikely to yield much insight. Instead, iterating fast and tweaking different behaviours has greater impact. Experimentation and learning from failure are just as useful for behaviour change as for other company processes where iteration may be traditionally employed, such as lean start-up methodology.

Second, hacking deals with (even thrives on) constraints or limitations. On an organizational level, a typical constraint may be lack of budget or time, which nevertheless drives people to more crea-tive solutions. On a personal level constraints are also present. For example, in a busy life it may be hard to retain focus or attention on habits, or there may be such variation in your day-to-day that it is hard to see where new habits could be placed. For health-centric habits such as going to the gym or cooking more, you may simply not have the time.

Finally, we believe hacking should produce unconventional solu-tions. Challenging conventional wisdom is important. This could be driven by the other two elements. For example, instead of trying to carve out time to go to the gym twice a week, try suggesting a walking or even running meeting with a client to discuss that next project. Over-long, inefficient meetings killing energy in your team? Get rid of the chairs and cut the normal meeting time in half.

In essence, hacking is about curiosity. Many articles on social media these days take the form of some personal experiment, say drinking water or exercising each day for a period of time and noting what happens. The content is often uninspiring, but the approach is not, and is reflective of what scientists have done for years: designing an experiment, measuring, and drawing conclusions. So hacking can be defined succinctly as acting like a scientist but without a budget!

Inspired by Covey, the following elements are the seven hacks of highly effective habits. They are the result of a decade of executive teaching and research.

The seven hacks of highly effective habits

1. Small

The typical approach to change, particularly by the driven pro-fessional class, is that of a significant effort towards achieving an ambitious or stretch goal. By definition, this significant effort is deployed now and again, which may or may not lead to success. Yet a much smaller (and therefore more sustainable) effort on a daily basis is likely to yield a greater benefit. Daily implementation is key. We highlighted the Maxwell quote of changing our lives through daily action in chapter eight, and to that train of thought we can also add Gretchen Rubin, another American author, who said that: "What you do everyday matters more than what you do every once in a while."

A very successful habit may exist of course on a less frequent level, yet the daily implementation means that the cumulative benefit will quickly accrue for a relatively minor effort. The lauded strategy of 'the cumulative effect of marginal gains' from the British Olympic track-cycling team shows how even tiny changes allied to accumulation can have a big impact – in their case, from being a mediocre performer winning one Olympic gold in 100 years, to becoming the sport's preeminent force, with 22 gold medals in the last three Olympic Games. Their marginal gains included rubbing the tyres of the bicycles with alcohol after each round of competition to remove particles of dust, examining the official bus timetable and contracting their own transport company to give the cyclists 15 minutes more rest in the Olympic village, and asking a leading surgeon to show the cyclists how to wash their hands, so as to minimize the chances of catching a cold or virus. In our business coaching work we've been inspired by marginal gains and have seen the impact of small changes, such as improving executives' ability to sleep on a plane by making use of their own pillow.

Making it small also increases the chances of creating a new habit, since it gains 'automaticity' in less time. Researchers at University College London found the amount of time for behaviours of varying complexity to become automatic ranged from 18 to 254 days.[2] For example, as shown in the figure below, creating the habit of drinking a glass of water took much less time than doing 50 sit-ups, with the authors finding a plateau to be reached, on average, after 66 days.

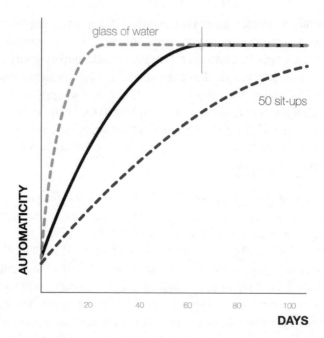

Figure 10.1. Time to achieve automaticity for different tasks

2. Specific

As ambition derails many attempts at successful behaviour change, so too does vagueness. Setting SMART (specific, measurable, agreed-upon, realistic, time-based) objectives helps to achieve professional targets and the same detail-oriented approach can help on a personal level.

Set a finish line. Rather than making an open commitment to always take the staircase, start with a commitment to always take the staircase for the remainder of the month. Achieving your objective will give you the motivation to keep going.

Given the daily approach mentioned above, another key detail is when in the day you will commit to change. Consider your own life as well as your daily biological rhythm and biochemistry, as we covered in chapter eight. Knowing that willpower tends to decrease throughout the day should be considered. Committing to something early in the day works for many, yet another slot may be required if family or other matters take precedence. In any case, try and fix the same time each day – which leads to the next S.

3. Supported

Support your new action by placing it next to an existing one. What do you do each day? Perhaps you have a consistent routine related to your morning: personal hygiene or preparing kids for school. Do some squats after brushing your teeth (or during!) Triggers can be immensely powerful. Stanford educator and behaviour-change expert B. J. Fogg talks of his "flushing the toilet" trigger, after which he would complete a couple of push-ups. Though perhaps not for every one (and he did stress only at home!), it is a much easier way of doing 20 to 30 push-ups on a daily basis than all at once.

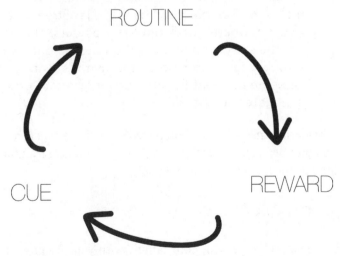

Figure 10.2. The habit cycle

Triggers give us a broader view of the behaviour and make it easier to implement, or displace, through considering the habit loop. A cue or signal exists before the habit, which then produces a reward. Rather than focusing on the behaviour itself, can you change the cue or reward? One of our coaching clients had a long-term bad habit of checking their email and social media in bed before going to sleep. After our coaching conversations, we identified the cue as them having their smartphone plugged to a charging cable on the bedside table. We eliminated the cue by placing the charging cable in the kitchen. The executive later told us they still wanted to check their phone in bed many evenings, but the cue was no longer there.

Considering the habit loop in its entirety also shifts the focus from the 'hard' routine to the much easier cue. Once we enter into the process we're committed to follow-through. The dancer and choreographer Twyla Tharp shows an example of this from her 2003 book, *The Creative Habit*:

> "I begin each day of my life with a ritual: I wake up at 5.30am, put on my workout clothes, my leg warmers, my sweatshirts, and my hat. I walk outside my Manhattan home, hail a taxi, and tell the driver to take me to the Pumping Iron gym at 91st Street and First Avenue, where I work out for two hours. The ritual is not the stretching and weight training I put my body through each morning at the gym; the ritual is the cab. The moment I tell the driver where to go I have completed the ritual."

Considering the task to be completed as calling a taxi (especially the night before), rather than two hours of physical training also lightens the mental load considerably.

4. Shared

Share your change with your family, with your friends, or with your boss. If you plan to go offline after a certain time each day, you'll need to manage expectations on a professional level. If you have a habit of collapsing on the sofa when you arrive home from work, tell your family so they are waiting for you to go for a walk when you arrive home. Sharing your change makes you accountable. And we all need to be held accountable.

The power of the coaching process also exists in creating this accountability, between coach and coachee. In the workplace, adding 'bottom-up' to the usual 'top-down' accountability has much potential. Leaders are often gauged on their credibility by matching their actions to their words. By sharing your own critical behaviours with your team you are creating a healthy pressure to follow through.

Telefónica CEO José María Álvarez-Pallete is a habitual Twitter user. The habit itself isn't so much the use of Twitter, rather the practice of daily reading that he finds so valuable, and which he subsequently communicates via the social media platform. Daily Twitter use for a CEO of a publicly traded company which employs over 130,000 people would of course have its drawbacks, yet the value of the daily reading habit outweighs any disadvantages. He spends around 25-30 minutes reading different articles as soon as he arrives at the office, before programming an average of ten tweets per day.[3] We could say he is held accountable for his daily reading habit by the almost 64,000 followers he has on Twitter, with whom he shares his activity each day.

5. Streak

Tracking the completion, or absence, of a certain behaviour over time creates a chain. And the longer that chain is, the harder it can be to break. This may be true of certain bad habits we have had for a long time, such as smoking. Alcoholics Anonymous, with its original *Big Book* – first published in 1939, is rich source of insight on behaviour for the public at large, and uses total sobriety time as a part of open group sharing.

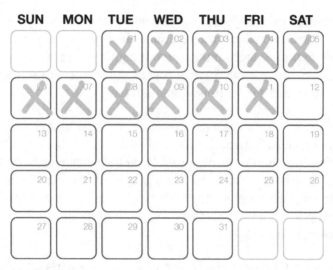

Figure 10.3. Maintaining a streak

Yet the same logic can be used in a positive sense, for example, winning streaks in sport. It is also used in many apps today. For example, one may achieve special badges for maintaining a streak of daily practice such as meditation. If you have a bad day after 150 days of completing the same practice and the last thing on your mind is meditation, the simple fact of having completed 150 days will probably get you over the line to complete 151. An extreme example comes from the former British Olympic marathon runner Ron Hill. In January of 2017, at age 78, he brought to an end 19,032 consecutive days of running at least one mile. Again, we may imagine that on many occasions during those 52-plus years he may not have wanted to run, with the power of the streak the only thing of relevance. While running sick and with chest pains on the final day of the streak he felt it unfair on his family to continue, so decided to bring the streak to an end.

Think of the power of such streaks in sectors like health and safety in construction. If you are a worker on such a site, with a visible counter that says: "1,068 days since last accident", that's a powerful incentive not to be the one who brings the counter back to zero.

6. Surroundings

In an increasingly digital world, the physical environment matters more than ever. It is a powerful determinant of our behaviour, and one which we look at in greater detail in the next chapter.

Consider for example your home environment and perhaps a commitment to a morning yoga routine. One of the keys to building this into the daily routine would be to have the yoga mat in plain view. That way, rather than blearily fetching coffee as part of your daily stumble out of bed, unfurling that mat is a more natural part of the daily flow. It's a similar, even simpler principle to that of laying out your workout clothes the night before an early-morning training session.

At work, simple changes could include a standing desk, new vending machine content, or simple changes to the staircase in order to make it more inviting. You may not have the reported $5 billion that Apple spent on its new spaceship campus but we can all think about redesigning our surroundings to support behaviour change and nudge both ourselves and our teams to implement the critical few behaviours that support an improved culture.

Figure 10.4. Staircase nudge from The Leadership Academy of Barcelona

Google has considered a behavioural economics approach in redesigning its own workplace environment. In a look at how employees snacked throughout the day, it was found that the location matters in a coffee area, with workers 50% more likely to take a snack with a cup of coffee when the snacks are three metres closer.[4] We are also drawn to variety as human beings, with people tending to eat fewer M&Ms from a bowl of the same colour, even though all M&Ms taste the same. Such an approach integrates some of our content of chapter nine, particularly observation, with the experimentation advocated here.

7. Social

Jim Rohn said "we are the average of the five people we spend the most time with". What we often perceive to be our own behaviours are due to the influence of our family, friends, and colleagues. Thinking of our social environment will allow us greater insight to the habit-hacking process. Think of who you spend time with, both personally and professionally. Who are the people that will help you most in the formative stages of a new behaviour?

We may also think of our leadership activity and the design of teams. Research has shown the positive impact of placing a poor performer next to a high performer, with positive 'spillovers' created in terms of productivity, effectiveness, and client satisfaction with the work.[5] The authors suggest pairing employees with opposite strengths, as well as separating toxic workers.

Are all 7Ss to be employed in each case? Probably not. That is part of the habit-hacking process: finding out which ones are most important for you to gain traction in behaviour change, either to create and sustain a new healthy habit, or stop a more negative one in its tracks. We discuss below which of the seven hacks have proven most successful with participants on our executive education programmes.

We are the average of the five people we spend the most time with.

The key is to keep it simple. We are inundated with a barrage of daily clickbait – often list-heavy articles that proclaim for example: "14 things that successful people do before breakfast." *The Economist* took a swipe at such pieces a few years ago and made a call to take a step back from such frenetic hyperactivity and the growing cult of the 'superboss'.[6] We believe a more relaxed yet curious approach to understanding one's own behaviour, along the lines of hacking as described above, will result in greater insight to our subconscious selves and the identification of those keystone habits that make the rest of our lives function better, as well as our places of work.

Our research on habits at Telefónica

We have looked to gain greater insight into habits in the workplace through our research with attendees at Universitas Telefónica.[7] We were interested first of all in where and when habits were implemented, and what effects this placement had on the success of the habit. All attendees at the university during 2016 were surveyed, a total of 1,900 senior managers, with 574 responses received.

The results of the placement of habits are shown below and reflect our expectations – that respondents would be more comfortable attempting behaviour change at home. There is approximately an 80/20 split between home and work habits, with a more even distribution between morning (53% of sample) and evening (47% of sample).

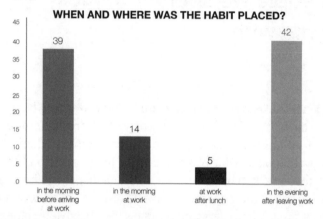

Figure 10.5. Habit placement for 2016 data (sample = 574)

The success of habit formation, shown below, produced one or two surprises. Although we see success (as expected in line with our understanding of circadian rhythms) in the morning, what we didn't expect was the most successful slot to be at work after lunch. This is the smallest part of the sample, but still worthy of further reflection.

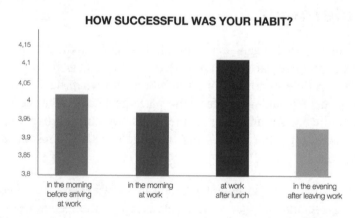

Figure 10.6. Subjective evaluation of habit formation success

It could be that lunch has provided an additional energy boost for habit effort, consistent with some of the work in the decision-fatigue field. Perhaps also, with work priorities having been taken care of in the morning, the afternoon allows more space for thinking about self-improvement. In any case, we see an opportunity for greater attention to habits in the work environment, where only 20% of our sample chose to place them. With increasing attention to workplace design, an accompanying belief from the employee that their work environment offers a supportive space for positive behaviour change may impact greatly on workplace wellbeing.

As part of our ongoing analysis we are interested to find out if any of the variables positively predict successful behaviour change. These variables include gender, nationality, whether the change is targeted in the morning, and when the response data was entered in our collection form. This last variable is the most interesting as we have used it as a proxy for inferring the person's chronotype (that is their lark or owl profile, as discussed in chapter eight). What we have found is that morning people have a higher level of success in forming the new behaviour compared to non-morning people (4.3 versus 3.5) and that the difference is statistically significant ($p < 0.01$). This seems to be consistent with the published research into morningness-eveningness, and we are excited to advance this avenue in our ongoing work.

Our research with attendees to Universitas during 2017, again with a total potential sample of around 2,000, looks at which of the seven hacks are most effective. All attendees attended a short Habit Hacking module comprised of two sessions, which covered the seven hacks and discussed how they could implement them in their lives. At the time of going to press we have received and processed the first 100 responses, with preliminary analysis as follows.

As with the 2016 sample, self-reported evaluations of habit success tend towards the upper end of the scale, with an overall average of 3.7/5, with 5 being the most successful. We would like to think our interventions are so effective that they result in a high degree of success, but have to acknowledge that the more likely explanation is that some people give themselves a higher score than the reality – perhaps not willing to fully accept their own 'failure' in a task. A further factor could be the time of survey, around the 100-day mark after the initial intervention, which may still represent the successful startup phase. Surveying the same people, for example, one year later would provide an interesting picture as to how sustainable their change really was. In any case, there is an even balance between those selecting 1, 2, and 3 out of 5, the 'poor performers' (49%) and 4 and 5, the 'high performers' (51%), which will allow further analysis.

The level of usage and success of each of the seven hacks allows further insight. Small is by far the most commonly used tactic, with 74% of the sample using that particular hack. We note that it does have the privileged position of being the first on the list, in both the training interventions and 100-day survey. It had a slightly above-average score, with people who used it, having an average success rating of 3.8/5. The most effective hacks are Streak and Surroundings, which each had an average score of 4.0 for those who used them.

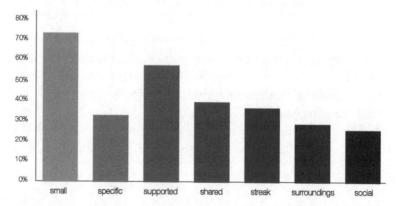

Figure 10.7. Level of use of each of the seven hacks

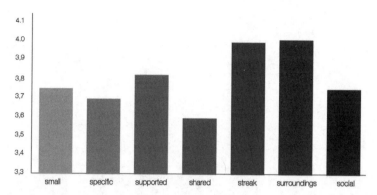

Figure 10.8. Average score (effectiveness) of each of the seven hacks

A final reflection regards the overall tactics used by the best and worst performers. Those who rated the top five for habit formation used an average of 3.3 different hacks. 4/5 used an average of 3.0. Those who had the lowest scores, 1 and 2, used a total of 2.6 and 2.0 hacks respectively. This would seem to suggest that success is predicted by a larger number of hacks in use. One possible explanation could be that more hacks present different options for a changing personal and professional context, in order to stay the course with behaviour change. We are continuing to collect data and analyse both the 2016 and 2017 samples in order to test this and the other insights noted above.

Data analytics are helping us to understand patterns of behaviour on a deeper level, and can throw up some surprises. Barcelona is home to the fourth-biggest passenger port in the world, after the three in Florida. A total of four million people visit the city's port each year, and it was also home for the inaugural season of the largest passenger ship in the world, *Harmony of the Seas,* with a capacity of up to 9,000 people. A boon for the city, as those up-wardly-mobile tourists spend their disposable income here, right? Until you consider that upwards of 30% of the people never actu-ally get off the boat.[8] Identifying behavioural patterns is a major benefit of our big-data era, but changing that behaviour remains a significant challenge. Addressing discrete habits on a very human level may help.

11

ENVIRONMENTAL
DESIGN

"You take the blue pill – the story ends, you wake up in your bed and believe whatever you want to believe. You take the red pill – you stay in Wonderland and I show you how deep the rabbit-hole goes."

Morpheus, *The Matrix*

THE AIRBUS A380 is the largest passenger aeroplane in the world. At 73m long and 80m wide, the double-deck, wide-body jet can carry over 850 passengers in an economy-class-only configuration. Many of the airports around the world had to upgrade their facilities to deal with a machine twice as long as a blue whale and containing more than 500km of wiring. And for a while it seemed that this engineering marvel was not going to make it to Barcelona all because of some ducks.

The new Barcelona Airport Terminal One building (the fifth largest in the world) and a third runway were opened in 2009, yet the original plans had designed a much longer runway. In the end, it had to be shortened since it was pushing up against a protected wildlife area. The irony is that the lakes are artificial – when they built the airport, they had to get sand and rocks for the construction from the surrounding area. Then it rained and the birds from the Llobregat Delta on the other side of the airport moved in.

We think this provides an important lesson for businesses and their actions towards looking after the people within them. No matter how bold your ambitions, with the requisite resources in place, the most talented people may flounder unless the right environment is provided to support their work. Two of the seven hacks we detailed in the previous chapter concern the environment; Surroundings and Social, and we detail them further in this chapter. The aim is to provide a guide on designing the right environment for workplace wellbeing.

The company environment

Too many business environments are sterile. Clinical. Devoid of emotion. Too often the new open-plan office which was so well-intended and created for open dialogue and team interactivity, merely suffocates authentic emotional behaviour. Nobody dares to make a noise. Nobody has any private space to exclaim, shout, or cry. Even if you cough or sneeze, heads will turn with possible sneers. In all, emotions are dampened and individuality is further eroded.

Furthermore, in the absence of any regular zone that is yours in the age of the hot desk, where you may be sitting down at any cubicle on any floor and have nowhere to call your own, recent studies show reduced productivity and increased unease. Nobody has any safe territory. They always feel exposed. No wonder people increasingly wish to work from home, which may improve efficiency, but it's incredibly hard to bond a geographically distributed team that hardly ever comes together. Google famously does the opposite. It will do anything to encourage people to stay at work: people own their space, live at the office, bring their pets to work, exercise and eat at work. It's not for everyone, though it does create cohorts of enthusiastic Googlers.

THE STANFORD PRISON EXPERIMENT

The idea that the environment you find yourself in, the power you are given, as well as the systems and processes provided to you, can quickly change you as a human being is clearly illustrated by the famous Stanford Prison experiment. In 1971 the US Navy sponsored an experiment led by psychology professor Philip Zimbardo to investigate this, and to specifically try to understand the dysfunctional relationship between prisoners and their guards. They wanted to understand what made a guard abusive: was it his inherent personality traits or was it the environment he found himself in?

They selected healthy, middle-class college students and they divided them up into guards and prisoners. They then 'arrested' those that had been selected as prisoners, strip-searched them, gave them prison uniforms, and put them into fake cells in the basement of the psychology department at Stanford. Guards were told not to physically harm the 'prisoners' but were given wooden batons and encouraged to make the prisoners feel as uncomfortable and disoriented as possible, and with no privacy. Prisoners were relieved of their names and referred to only as numbers. They made it clear that the guards had the power and the prisoners had none.

After less than two days one prisoner went 'crazy' and had to be let out. After that, the other prisoners began to show warning signs of mental and physical deterioration. At the same time the guards turned into sadistic megalomaniacs. They were abusive and cruel, and even gave themselves more authority than the roles originally prescribed to them. Their humanity seemed to have been removed, and after only six days of abusing their power the experiment had to be discontinued.

The experiment seemed to prove that one's role and environment can very quickly erode one's character, values, and humanity. This is what happens in many companies today. Instead, we need to celebrate the unique character traits of every one of a company's employees, and not allow them to be eroded, flattened, and swallowed by the system. We detect social and physical aspects of the environment in the Stanford Prison experiment, which we look at now in turn.

Designing the physical environment

Apple Park opened in April 2017 and will eventually provide a working base to 12,000 employees. The new headquarters of one of the world's most innovative companies, referred to by many as 'spaceship campus' due to its flying saucer-like design, was one of the final acts from Steve Jobs before he passed away in 2011. The building is aimed at encouraging collaboration and will provide employees with opportunities to run into each other and interact, reflective of Jobs' decision in 2000 to scrap plans for three separate buildings at Pixar in favour of one vast atrium-type space. The spaceship will contain a lake, meadow, and orchard within its inner ring, while also offering a 9,290 square metre fitness centre and 3km of walking and running paths across the 175-acre site.

Leading companies around the world are waking up to the fact that physical space matters more than ever. There is a growing realization that the modern workplace is no longer just seen as the desk, but also, and probably more importantly, the area around it. The growing premium on creative work from the workforce at large requires a new type of environment, something alluded to when IDEO's Tom Kelley observed that "when I see someone at their desk all day it's suspicious how they pretend to work".

As we experience profound changes in the world of work and how it fits within our lives, emerging notions of space – supporting positive behaviour, health and wellness, dynamic interaction, and providing options for different configurations – will be present in the leading organizations of the future, regardless of size or sector. Today, we can work from anywhere at any time, yet the design of the physical space will play an increasingly important role in the future of work.

Today's workplace design goes beyond traditional conversations around open- and closed-plan layouts to incorporate aspects of biophilic design, better-quality air and working options to combat sedentarism.

The last decade has seen significant growth in the awareness of environmentally-conscious building design, supported by increasing implementation of green building standards such as LEED. LEED, which stands for Leadership in Energy and Environmental Design, is the most widely used green building-rating system in the world, with buildings gaining points for different features and rated from Certified to Platinum. Strategies to improve human health and wellbeing have played a relatively minor role over the same period, but we view the next decade as being pivotal to that integration, which we believe will go hand in hand with green building design. What is good for the planet is often also good for us all as human beings, and vice versa. When we consider that we spend, on average, 90% of our time inside a building it is only a matter of time before the current societal trend of considering the importance of human health on all levels extends to the building design industry.

So how would an organization get started with improvements in the physical space? Different checklists and standards now exist, which we cover below, but simply starting by remembering we are flesh and bones is key, as noted by Dr. Francesca Mastrogiacomi, former head of learning design for Google's Digital Academy in

EMEA and now founder of Creative [X] Factory in Italy. She has her own checklist for the workspace, which includes elements of "windows, fresh air, green space, daylight, plants, cozy areas, comfy corners, silent spaces, and noisy coffee corners", believing that the learning journey is improved when people move, stand up, get outside, walk, and talk.

Remembering our human nature again points to the value of a design-thinking approach. We believe the whole process of healthy building design and construction needs to be fuelled at the front-end by human-centred design, in order to support wellbeing and quality creative work. Rather than architects designing what they think will fit the organization on a general level, perhaps as a result of industry trends, technological developments or what worked with other clients, a deep-dive is required to look at the existing working patterns of the workforce, current pain points and a true understanding of employee needs, facilitated by on-site observation, semi-structured interviews, accidental conversations, and prototyping. Only this experience-design approach will allow the generation of non-obvious insights that feed the traditional architecture and build phase of a new space.

Table 11.1. Traditional vs design-thinking approach to building design

	Traditional building design	**Human-centred design-thinking**
Approach	What has worked elsewhere	What is required here
Input	Demographics, available technology	Observed behaviour
Understanding employees	Scripted transcripts	Dynamic conversations
Experimental space	Controlled setting	Natural context

Some basics of a design-thinking approach were employed at Alpha, Telefónica's long-term innovation lab and moonshot factory in Barcelona. Ironically for a company whose first moonshot is in health and behaviour change, the team's own health was being compromised while in startup mode. It was cramped in a small space, and mobility during the day was minimal, enforced by an intensive small-team startup culture, where people worked long hours and ordered food in. The office overlooks Barceloneta beach, yet walking meetings along the Mediterranean rarely ever happened.

HR director David Armengol examined current patterns by setting up a video camera and tracking movement over a number of days. Some of the insights were used in the design of a new larger space. Armengol stated that "we thought about the flow of people during the working day and decided on simple features, including the use of hot desking, lockers, and a larger kitchen and eating area. We were also keen to maintain a balance between visibility and privacy, whether for the individual or team meeting." Our own engagement and experiments with the team there aimed to leverage the increased comfort and suitability of the larger space, so that actually leaving it and getting outside was a more natural proposition.

Such a process may seem simple and obvious, yet even the leading companies in the world sometimes make mistakes. In spite of a slew of unique and advanced features in Apple's spaceship campus to make the employee experience as good as possible (even including special entryways that mean people needn't slow their pace as they enter), reports emerged in August 2017 of an extreme dislike for the new open-plan spaces, where engineers are expected to work at long tables instead of having their own office or module.[1] We assume such issues will iron themselves out over time as the employees find a new work dynamic that allows them to move between private and public spaces, yet this story shows that even by spending $5 billion, the most basic of office design dilemmas still remain. It would be interesting to find out to what extent Apple employees, and the different teams in charge of different divisions, were consulted in the process, and if the very design process that has proved so valuable in the company's products, was used in the design of its new headquarters.

A useful design method to look closer at specific requirements is that of extreme user analysis – analysing the needs of some extreme population outside your own domain to provide inspiration for your own context. If we think which sector has an extreme need for their occupants to have better physical and mental health and wellbeing, the healthcare sector itself would seem a good candidate.

Human-centred design consultants are an increasingly-used resource by hospitals and healthcare facilities. A better understanding of specific patient needs has been exploited, for example, in the redesign of healthcare provision for young children. Changes to equipment including MRI scanners can alter what can be a highly daunting experience to something that is fun and connects with the playful nature of children (see photo below).

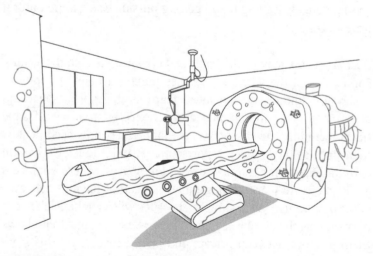

Figure 11.1. A children's MRI scanning room

The provision of nature, and natural elements in particular, has been shown to improve the physical and mental health of patients. Until relatively recently in human history, people had constant interaction with living things and their natural surroundings. Biophilia is the idea that humans have a natural affinity with the natural world. Interior environments that are cold, sterile, and devoid of life can diminish our health, mood, and happiness.

Research has shown hospital patients to recover more quickly when exposed to natural light from a window, while other studies show workspaces that incorporate natural elements report a 15% higher level of wellbeing, 6% higher level of productivity, and a 15% higher level of creativity.[2] Biophilic design principles may therefore provide significant benefit for both patients and employees alike. In the office environment, research has shown that adding houseplants to an otherwise sparse space can increase wellbeing by 47%, increase creativity by 45%, and increase productivity by 38%.[3]

Mental wellbeing in a healthcare setting may also provide food for thought. IDEO redesigned the waiting rooms for Planned Parenthood in the US, a network of clinics offering a range of services for sexual and reproductive health. Patients were known to experience significant nervousness and fear from certain members of society as well as the healthcare provision itself. For example. Pro-Life campaigners would often harass visitors to what they viewed simply as an abortion clinic with even a fatal shooting occurring in 2015. Patient safety and empathy were therefore key drivers in the process. Some of the design features implemented include:

- Combination seating, offering patients the choice of a relaxed communal table or more private 'pods'.

- Good-quality lighting to help combat nervousness and fear, and bright airy colours in general.

- Seating with a view of the reception area, as people like to see what's going on and feel 'updated' during the waiting process.

- Information apps as a type of 'visit companion', with FAQ and information on the patient procedure and treatment.

In the building checklist and standards space, researchers at the London School of Economics created the SALIENT checklist as a means of improving wellbeing and also influencing positive behaviour. In applying the framework to an Accident and Emergency waiting area in an NHS hospital in the UK, music was found to increase calmness among study participants, with artwork also shown to help with pain reduction.

The elements and key insights of SALIENT are as follows:

- SOUND: Our attention is drawn to unpredictable and attention-seeking sounds.

- AIR: We are affected by air-flow, temperature, source, and scents.

- LIGHT: Our behaviour is influenced by the source and brightness of light.

- IMAGE: We are stimulated by certain imagery and affected by clutter.

- ERGONOMICS: We do not adapt well to poorly designed furniture and equipment.

- NATURE: We are affected in largely positive ways by exposure to natural elements.

- TINT: Our behaviour is affected by the presence of different colours.

Moving beyond a simple checklist is the Well Building Standard, as maintained by the International Well Building Institute.[4] This is the result of several years' development by dozens of scientists worldwide. Well aligns with current green building standards, including LEED, and is comprised of 100 separate features divided into the seven categories of air, water, nourishment, light, fitness, comfort, and mind. These features vary from the highly technical, associated with architectural and engineering design (such as the measurement of air quality) to areas that affect HR policy and things such as mindful eating. Each feature is targeted at improving human health according to 11 different biological systems, including the cardiovascular system, digestive system, and endocrine system.

Growing interest in the Well Building Standard is accompanied by an evolving ecosystem of innovative startups worldwide. One such company is Naava, co-founded by Finnish entrepreneur Aki Soudunsaari. Inspired by Aki's own upbringing in the idyllic natural environment of Northern Finland, Naava creates natural green walls to improve the air quality of buildings, in order to combat what it sees as one of the most serious health risks worldwide. Biophilic design is at the core of what Naava does and it believes that, from a genetic standpoint, we are no different from the hunter-gatherers of 40,000 years ago and are meant to live in nature (see figure 11.2).

From a genetic standpoint, we are no different from the hunter-gatherers of 40,000 years ago and are meant to live in nature.

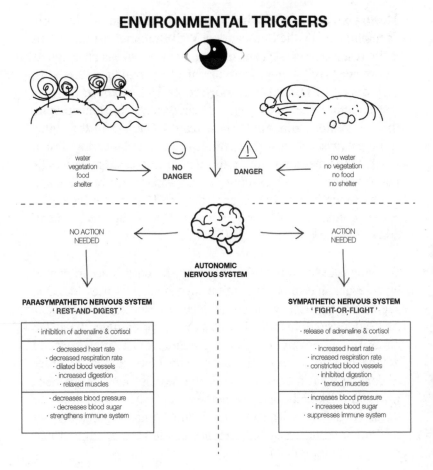

Figure 11.2. Environmental triggers from Naava (naava.io)

The fact that our core biology and human needs haven't changed much in that time explains many of the stress-related illnesses and effects on our nervous system that we touched on in chapter eight, when discussing circadian rhythm. Even simple changes to the physical environment, together with many of the other personal actions we detail in *Chief Wellbeing Officer* will help reconnect us to our true human selves and improve health, wellbeing, and performance.

A case from professor MacGregor

Rubén Galcerán is the head of Global Workspace Solutions at CBRE Spain. His office in Barcelona is the first to be certified in both LEED and WELL from the design phase. He believes that both complement one another to ensure that the building preserves the energy and precious resources of the planet as well as the people who work there. Though many building occupiers today are on-board with sustainability certification such as LEED or BREEAM, Galcerán sees world-class companies starting to recognize the strategic importance and advantage of wellbeing. He also sees increasing wellbeing demand from employees, which not only contribute to improving employee satisfaction and productivity, but also in improved talent attractiveness and retention. In fact, according to the latest CBRE global report, 85% of young employees recognize wellbeing at their workplace as a key factor.

He details that: "WELL certification makes CBRE Barcelona a space committed to the health, wellbeing, and comfort of its employees, through best practices, both in design and construction. This is reflected in some of the measures implemented, such as low-emissive materials, optimum ventilation rates and filters, fresh and healthy produce, ergonomic and active furniture, low-noise equipment and fitness activities, among others. Design and technology strategies have been defined to provide a physical environment that is able to optimize mental and cognitive health by incorporating vegetation and art into the workspace." The results obtained from the implementation of these measures have resulted in considerable savings of energy (12%), water consumption (40%), and printing (25%) for the company, as well as a 30% increase in productivity and 76% increase in employee satisfaction. In addition, having innovative and healthy offices has contributed to the company's inclusion in the Best Place to Work ranking, which recognizes the 50 best companies to work for in Spain.

Physical environments therefore influence how people feel and provide signals about how to behave. Such 'nudging' and the use of behavioural economics links closely to the human-centred approach to building design that we advocate here. In this way, leaders can help make the emotional parts of a space as important as the functional, and thereby promote a sense of purpose and belonging among employees. Emotional wellbeing is improved by the physical environment, but we must also consider the social.

Designing the social environment

The individual view

A common thread in the self-management and coaching domain is reflecting on who we spend time with. Advice, some of which we covered in chapter three, ranges from being careful with people who are a drain on your energy through their negative attitude, to simply saying no to requests for your time. Surrounding yourself with enthusiastic, inspirational people, and indulging in more interesting conversations with them can make a significant difference to your own energy. It can also positively influence any negative traits or complaints that come in to your own language and behaviour.

In the previous chapter we highlighted the Jim Rohn quote that "we are the average of the five people we spend the most time with". Whether this exposure to other people's behaviours, opinions, and habits is face-to-face or online through social media, we will be influenced by it and likely assimilate more than we realize. Taking a key area of focus from the social media world, this exposure could be termed our 'feed'.

For companies such as Facebook, much of what they do comes down to feed. Design decisions, client engagement for selling ads, user attraction, and audio and video habits are all related. And it's true of all social media channels. The feed is what promotes use and those repeat visits (often hundreds) during the week. More time spent on the feed means more revenue to the leading tech companies. Our behaviour is greatly affected by and through this feed. It is part of our social environment.

Persuasive psychology principles are used to grab your attention and keep it. The alarming thing is that several dozen designers living in California and working at just a few companies are impacting the lives of over a billion people around the planet. And spending increasing amounts of time scrolling through feeds on different channels isn't the best thing for health, wellbeing, or performance. Think about your own habits in the past year or two, and how any changes in behaviour, and specifically spending increasing amounts of time with your feed, have made you feel.

There is another element of feed that affects our behaviour. We design our own feed (though heavily influenced by those several dozen designers). We connect with friends and colleagues we like, and follow companies and public figures we admire. And the source of this attraction and connection often stems from some similarity that we see in them – we may hold the same values or opinions, come from the same place, or work for the same company. Maybe we like the same music, support the same football team, or believe in the same causes or politics. Our feed gives us a world view that is anything but worldly. It is segmented and we are blindsided to the opinions, values, preferences, and affiliations of those we don't connect with. We need not look any further than the surprise election of Donald Trump in 2016 to show how our customized feeds lead us to believe how one set of events will unfold. In the final days of the election campaign *The New York Times* predicted the probability of a Clinton win at over 90%.

Another interesting political story from history shows how our feed can exist in different areas of our life, not just online. In the year 1929, and nearing the end of his second, ill-fated term as the president of Argentina, Hipólito Irigoyen began to receive filtered news from his closest aides. The Great Depression was having a devastating impact throughout Latin America, and the country was sliding inexorably into crisis. Highlighting only good news and passing over some of the more negative events in presidential communication, no matter how slight that actually was, was exaggerated greatly, leading to one of Argentina's most popular myths: that a special newspaper was printed for Irigoyen which included only good news. *El Diario de Irigoyen* or Irigoyen's Daily, is a well-known phrase in Argentina to this day, and used when people want to push back against a sugar-coated version of events.

Parallels with today are unmistakable. Putting aside recent reports that President Trump only likes to receive good news and that his aides have their own special way of communicating to him, never mind the growing controversy around fake news, we are each surrounded by our own version of *El Diario de Irigoyen,* on and offline.

So how may we push back against this and redesign our feed? Start with breaking out of autopilot and try a simple exercise. Take a look at the social media feed of another person – maybe your partner or (if they let you!) your children. Perhaps even a close colleague at work. Instantly, it will give you a slightly broader view that also seems more vibrant due to its differences. Perhaps you can also follow or at least check-in with accounts and people you would normally stay well clear of due to your differences.

How about having a higher percentage of your daily feed from offline sources? Actions with some of our coaching clients have included eliminating email from their phone (having access to email on other machines is more than enough when the person in question isn't travelling) and moving any feed-based apps out of the phone's home screen and into different folders to cut down on impulse checks.

How can you talk to people outside your usual network in order to broaden your perspective? In our client work we often encourage people to join a new club, as being held accountable by new people will help make habits stick. Forming new relationships, perhaps something we do less and less as we get older, helps change our views and perspectives. Even listening to those you vehemently disagree with is, we believe, a healthy exercise.

The organizational view

Many companies are guilty of removing the individual characteristics that make people human. They put employees into categories and are then surprised when performance actually correlates to the category they have been forced into. Cadres of so-called high performers ('Hi-Pos') appear and are invested in. How do you think this makes everybody else feel?

We should of course encourage excellence, but labels can be dangerous. Measurement systems are often unable to identify real high performance and excellence, and are more likely to highlight employees who play the game better. Employees may ask themselves, "If I'm not a Hi-Po', does that make me a Lo-Po? Am I useless?" This hardly encourages inspiration, creativity and initiative.

More recently, another group has been identified as 'Po-Pos'. These are the 'passed over and pissed-off' people. They are often cynical and disruptive, but they are survivors. They will be long in the company after the Hi-Pos have left. The whole thing resembles the donkey Benjamin in George Orwell's *Animal Farm*. Benjamin's famous cynical remark; "Donkeys live a long time. None of you has ever seen a dead donkey," reminds us how time and

In this way the company becomes great by celebrating diversity, rather than weak by encouraging sameness.

energy sapping these people can be unless they are encouraged. The point is that these donkeys, these Po-Pos, are likely to be just as intelligent as everybody else, just a bit cynical.

The company should be asking: how are we going to help these people? How are we going to leverage their unique intelligence and get them on to our side, rather than marginalizing them and creating a self-fulfilling prophecy of neglect, cynicism, and low performance – not unlike the Pygmalion effect we discussed in chapter three?

We detailed the importance of authenticity in chapter seven, and the key is to create an environment that allows employees to be themselves. Talent development should not be about filling skills gaps, but rather enhancing what skills and strengths people already have. In this way the company becomes great by celebrating diversity, rather than weak by encouraging sameness. It's all about creating an environment of trust, openness, and honesty, where emotions (laughing and crying) are encouraged and welcomed. If an employee wants to bring his mouse (or even super-rat) to work, then why not!

The physical and social environment contains a multitude of opportunities to improve wellbeing and work. We are shaped significantly by our environment in these two dimensions, and, in turn, help to shape it. We spend increasing amounts of time at work, mostly indoors, and the boundaries between work, rest, and play are increasingly blurred. Workspace design is a hot topic, yet some people may take a cynical view of the physical changes to squeeze more out of the employee if changes are not present also at the social level, including culture and leadership behaviour.

Remembering the Stanford Prison experiment, there's no doubt that many people's mental health is severely compromised at work. Different issues may be at play, yet a thorough consideration of environmental design, driven by the right process, will help address many, and is a critical piece of *Chief Wellbeing Officer*.

Both the natural and manufactured environments around Barcelona Airport continue to thrive. The birds of the Llobregat Delta seem not to have been overly inconvenienced by the arrival of the new super flying machine. Today, Les Filipines is one of the best beaches in Barcelona to go for a run – and we think the A380 which flies overhead at 3.30pm on its way to Dubai adds to the experience and spectacle of the natural environment. Just be aware that the local 'wildlife' also includes most of the nudist community of Barcelona!

12
LEADING IN
THE FUTURE
OF WORK

"Do. Or do not. There is no try."

Yoda, *Star Wars*

THE Carretera de les Aigües is a 10km track within the natural park of Collserola, which overlooks Barcelona. At 450m above sea level, its highest point affords spectacular views of the city very similar to those at the top of our secret staircase highlighted in chapter one. It also has the advantage of being a perfect running and cycling track, where we both do some of our best thinking and enjoy our deepest recovery. From here we can see the whole city, the big picture, and it gives us perspective on any challenges or problems we may be facing at the time.

Figure 12.1. Barcelona from Carretera de les Aigües

The view from the top

So what is the big picture for *Chief Wellbeing Officer*? We have attempted to make a convincing argument for a more human-driven approach to work, where wellbeing is a more strategic concern in the company. We believe this will be ever more critical in an emerging future that is digital, artificially intelligent, and always 'on'.

We started our journey by positing that now is the best time to be alive. We believe that to be the case but are conscious of the great challenges that face us individually and as a society. In many ways, we see the challenges as part of the great allure of living today, in so far as they are not insurmountable. We are provided like never before with tools, communication, awareness, and freedom to tackle these challenges head on.

We hope to have provided some tools and insights to tackle your own challenges through the three parts of this book. Part one attempted to set the scene for the world we live in today and the very different one that is just around the corner. Purpose, vision, and values were presented as the fundamental way in which we can bring a more human approach to leadership that delivers a

We have attempted to make a convincing argument for a more human-driven approach to work, where wellbeing is a more strategic concern.

return on investment in the areas that truly matter. Purpose has gained increasing attention in recent years, and with good reason. Think about your own friends, family, as well as public figures, and the effect that retirement, unemployment, empty-nest syndrome, or the end of a sports career has on their wellbeing.

Purpose allows us to find a path through disruption. Finding, defining, and honing our moral compass will allow us to navigate safely through a complex world. It will give you direction, inform you how to act, and help you know where you want to go and what the best version of 'you' looks like. Whatever is going on in the world, or in your country, company, team, family, or even in your own head, then the moral compass is the key element to guide you through the chaos and turbulence of life. It is personal, unique, and will help you prioritize what you should be doing right now and where you should be investing your valuable time. The moral compass enables you to distinguish things that are truly important from 'urgent' bullshit.

A story from Rory

My parents were Polar explorers. They saw no reason not to take their kids with them on their adventures. As such, me, my sister Rona and my two brothers Bruce and Robin, always went on their expeditions to the north. These included long summers in Greenland living with the Inuit (or Greenlanders as they prefer to be called), and canoe escapades in Alaska, Canada, Finland, and of course Scotland. The expeditions always had a purpose, which was somehow interwoven with my father's medical research and my mother's writing on adventure, family travel, and women's issues. Trips were funded by a wide range of interests and companies such as NASA, the US Air Force, The Daily Telegraph, and the BBC.

In the early summer of 1969 my parents set off for the North Pole. My siblings and I were left in an Inuit settlement and they headed even further north. Their objective was to be the first unsupported team to reach the Pole. All they had to do was to step off Ward Hunt Island in Northern Greenland on to the sea ice and keep going north! But it was not that easy. There was no GPS, and a compass doesn't work as you are already way past magnetic north, which lies near Ellesmere Island in Northern Canada at 81.3°N. Navigation was tough, especially as at that latitude there is only frozen sea that drifts. You may gain 80km in a day towards your destination, only to drift 100km in another direction. It seems like some kind of useful metaphor for daily life. Unless we are truly focused on something in particular then we will not get there. Unless we know exactly where we are going, and where we want to be, then we will not get there. Unless we can unload all the things that keep us from staying on track then we will not get there. It's about focus, unloading irrelevant emotional baggage, and having a clear objective or vision.

Professor Gretchen Spreitzer, a pioneering researcher in the area of thriving at work talked to us about more key elements, including the importance of connecting with others and providing the right environment – something we have addressed at different points. She said: "People get burned-out doing the same thing and want to build their purpose and have an impact."

This led us to consider two concepts from Japanese culture that have garnered interest in the West. First, that of *Ikigai*, which loosely translates to "a reason for being" and is the sweet spot of purpose and impact that leads to true wellbeing. We present this as a reminder that purpose doesn't always come easy. Some people may feel that they don't have one. Don't worry. Take your time and build towards it, as Spreitzer notes. Ikigai may provide a useful map to get there.

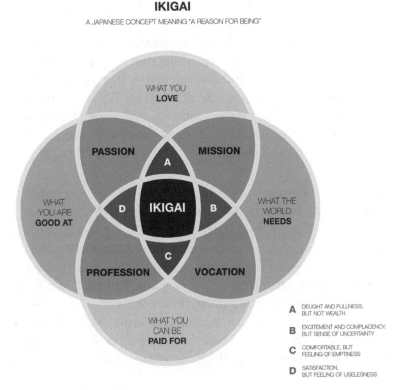

Figure 12.2. Ikigai

Yet danger lies in another Japanese word, that of *Karoshi*, or "death by overwork". This is an extreme case of burnout. Many Japanese regularly log over 100 hours overtime per month and can be found sleeping on the street, still suited and exhausted, between their place of work and home. It is a major problem for a country trying in vain to recapture the economic miracle of the 1960s to1980s. Not unlike other parts of Asia, depression and mental health issues are on the rise, and Ikigai remains an elusive dream for most. In Japan, Asia and the rest of the world will we follow the path to Ikigai or Karoshi? It's like the choice between the red pill and the blue pill in *The Matrix*. It's important to remember that it is a choice.

Time is a measure of the human capital we need to develop in the Fourth Industrial Revolution, yet it is only one measure. In part two we presented a more holistic way of perceiving performance, including total intelligence, circadian rhythms, and personal disruption that aligns with a more modern view of human capital that encompasses time, talent, and energy. We see both the business and moral case as inarguable – significant gains in talent and energy that result from considering these broader topics surely trump time on its own, no matter how much overtime is put in.

Some of the questions we raise have been posed for many years, and the Fourth Industrial Revolution may present the opportunity to answer them. Arnold Bennett, the English novelist and playwright published *How to Live on 24 hours a Day* in 1910. What he saw was an increasing number of white-collar workers simply 'existing' rather than truly living, as a result of the increasing work commitments of the (First) Industrial Revolution. Some of the advice he offers, such as finding pockets of time for self-development, as well as focused thinking time, are especially relevant more than 100 years later. He writes:

> "Which of us lives on 24 hours a day? And when I say 'lives', I do not mean exists, nor 'muddles through'. Which of us is free from that uneasy feeling that the 'great spending departments' of his daily life are not managed as they ought to be? [...] Which of us is not saying to himself – which of us has not been saying to himself all his life: 'I shall alter that when I have a little more time'? We never shall have any more time. We have, and we have always had, all the time there is."

We think Bennett would be fascinated by some of the findings of circadian rhythm science today and other research including that of Chris Barnes, a professor at the University of Washington. Barnes and colleagues have uncovered various insights on the link between sleep, chronotypes, and leadership, including the fact that larks working late at night tend to behave unethically, while owls working early in the morning do the same. In different studies[1] they have shown sleep deprivation to result in more abusive supervision, poorer quality of relationships and trust between manager and subordinate, and even less perception of charisma from the leader in question – those inspiring speeches therefore will only be well received by people who are well rested.

The contrast of the 24-hour day with the longer life and career in the Fourth Industrial Revolution highlights the key elements that drive personal disruption. Riding those S-curves may actually be fun if we pay closer attention to our total intelligence and daily biology.

Purpose, people, and passion need process to fully function. That is what we offer in part three, offering the structure and amplification of design-thinking. Process is key. As Picasso said, "Computers are useless, they can only give you answers." For the traditional application of new products and services, design makes knowledge and ideas tangible and concrete. For leadership, it makes a more human approach to work tangible and concrete. The design vowels give a voice to a more enlightened daily leadership practice.

The personal authenticity we present, and search for, in parts one and two, lands in this final part of the book with a look at behaviour. Identifying and changing those critical patterns through the seven hacks of highly effective habits, as well as a closer consideration of environment is now, we hope, a much easier proposition that will help deliver authenticity. Looking at behaviour also holds us accountable to the grand proclamations of purpose. Many companies today are guilty of 'purpose-washing' – jumping on the bandwagon of social impact, yet their daily operations and behaviours do nothing to back this up.

Do. Or do not

A key part of addressing new challenges is confronting fear. Fear of the unknown. Fear of failure. We have commented in previous chapters on using failure to our advantage, but regardless of any tactics used, it is still a scary and uncomfortable experience. Yet to improve our chances of sustained happiness, success, health, and wellbeing in our long lives and careers, we must be prepared to fail.

In many ways it doesn't matter how hard a new challenge is, or even if you fail. The hardest part is often making it to the start line. The moment the gun goes, you win. It is so easy to 'cop out' as we get older, and use the often very valid excuses not to do the things that are way outside our comfort zone. And further out of your comfort zone who is really going to judge you or hold you accountable if you don't follow through?

Embrace the fear. Look for firsts. Jump in. We tend to do less of this as we go through life, and many of the things that are so important in *Chief Wellbeing Officer* – navigating the cycles of change during our career, adopting a more human approach in our leadership practice, connecting with our physical and emotional selves, and redesigning our environment – require us to take such an approach.

To improve our chances of sustained happiness, success, health, and wellbeing in our long lives and careers, we must be prepared to fail.

Our time to do so is limited, of course. And time tends to move faster. American author Gretchen Rubin, writing in the context of happiness said that, "The days are long but the years are short." Savouring the moment, no matter how difficult that moment tends to be, is the takeaway message.

So why does time move faster? Marc Wittmann and Sandra Lenhoff, of Ludwig Maximilian University in Munich, surveyed 499 participants, ranging in age from 14 to 94 years, about the pace at which they felt time moving – from 'very slowly' to 'very fast'.[2] All respondents felt short time periods to pass in the same way, but those participants older than 40 felt long time periods, like decades, to pass quicker as they aged. This has been dubbed 'the holiday paradox' – our brain encodes new experiences, but not familiar ones, into memory, and our retrospective perception of time is based on how many new memories we create over a certain period. In other words, the more new memories we build during a holiday, the longer that trip will seem in hindsight.

This view builds on more wisdom from William James, who we visited in the context of habits in chapter ten. James noted that:

> "The shortening of the years as we grow older is due to the monotony of the memory's content and the consequent simplification of the backward-glancing view. Emptiness, monotony, and familiarity are what make time shrivel up."

Another theory on the passing of time relates to time as a function of the time we have already lived. This takes us from a linear view to the exponential, the scale on which we started our discussion in chapter one. To a two-year-old, a year is half of their life, which is why it seems such a long period of time to wait between birthdays. Car journeys seem endless for young children, prompting frequent requests as to the time of arrival. Our school summer vacations were endless, right? So for a ten-year-old, a year is 10% of their life and to a 20-year-old it is 5%. Using this logic, the following time periods would have the same perception: 5-10, 10-20, 20-40 and 40-80. Our aim is not to depress you by saying the 40 years until your 80th birthday will pass as quickly as your memories of moving from five to ten, but we do hope to provide a strong call to action.

Marcus Aurelius, that great Roman warrior and emperor spoke about happiness, choices, and of course philosophy. That was his guiding moral compass. Paraphrasing his words from *Meditations*, the classic compendium of his thought:

> "The duration of a person's life is only a moment; our substance is flowing away this very moment; the composition of the body is decaying. All bodily things are like a flowing river and everything of the soul is dream and smoke. And life is all warfare and a stranger's wanderings and the reward is oblivion. What then could possibly guide us? Only one thing: the moral compass of philosophy, and this consists of keeping the divine spirit within each of us free from disrespect and harm, above pains and pleasures, doing nothing aimlessly or falsely."

Putting aside the magnificent views and perspective that running and cycling on Carretera de les Aigües gives us, the biggest benefit is the range of paths presented to us. We may be travelling along the main path but by raising our gaze we are presented with myriad different paths and trails; up, down, narrow, and wide. They offer us new ways of arriving at the same destination or present us with a new end point. Often, they lead us to a dead-end and we need to backtrack. The joy is in the discovery. Getting lost and finding ourselves again. We hope you have enjoyed the path we have traced in *Chief Wellbeing Officer* and wish you the best, wherever that path leads you.

Embrace the fear.
Look for firsts.
Jump in.

REFERENCES/ NOTES

We have attempted to make most of our references, especially books, clear within each of the chapters to enable the reader to find the source of our inspiration. Where this is not the case we have included the citations below together with other supplemental notes.

Take Off

1 The World Economic Forum (WEF) have published several articles on The Fourth Industrial Revolution in the past few years. The following January 2016 article, written by WEF President Klaus Schwab would be a good starting point: https://www. weforum.org/agenda/2016/01/ the-fourth-industrial-revolution-what-it-means-and-how-to-respond/

2 The business and society case for Executive Health was the focus of the previous book written by Steven MacGregor: *Sustaining Executive Performance: How the New Self-Management Drives Innovation, Leadership, and a More Resilient World*, Pearson:NY, 2015.

3 C. B. Frey and M. Osborne, The Future of Employment: How susceptible are jobs to computerisation? Oxford Martin School, September 2013.

4 The quote comes from Michael Townsend Williams and is included in *The Stress Report*, a 2017 publication available for purchase at: http://www.thedolectures. com/shop/stressreport

5 Jones Lang Lasalle Global Report 2017 by Dr. Marie Puybaraud, available for download at: http://humanexperience.jll/ global-report/

Chapter 1

1 After the publication of these long-form Blog posts Tim Urban was commissioned by Elon Musk to write on Musk's companies

and surrounding industries. The first post which provides inspiration for us in Chapter 1 can be read here: https://waitbutwhy.com/2015/01/artificial-intelligence-revolution-1.html

2   This quote from Peter Thiel was written within a general critique on his perceived lack of ambition in the Venture Capital (VC) funding industry, published on his own VC company website. An overview of this critique together with link to his article can be found at the following link: http://www.businessinsider.com/founders-fund-the-future-2011-7

3   http://worldhappiness.report

4   High income improves evaluation of life but not emotional well-being, Daniel Kahneman and Angus Deaton, Proceedings of the National Academy of Sciences Sep 2010, 107 (38) 16489-16493; DOI: 10.1073/pnas.1011492107

5   http://www.un.org/sustainabledevelopment/sustainable-development-goals/

Chapter 2

1   Story of cities #13: Barcelona's unloved planner invents science of 'urbanisation', by Marta Bausells, 1st April 2016, The Guardian. Available online at: https://www.theguardian.com/cities/2016/apr/01/story-cities-13-eixample-barcelona-ildefons-cerda-planner-urbanisation

2   A popular Internet Infographic of the past few years has concerned the time taken for different technologies to reach 50 million users. Indeed, we commissioned a version to appear as one of the figures in this chapter. A common version will show the car is shown as taking 62 years, the Internet taking 7 years, Facebook 3 years and the popular app-based game Angry Birds a mere 35 days. However, the accuracy of these figures is highly debatable with little verifiable sources, hence its omission, yet it nonetheless shows the general dynamic that surrounds the diffusion of technology in a more globalized world.

3   We followed the commentary around small country effectiveness with particular interest leading up to the 2014 Scottish independence referendum. The Harvard Business Review Blog included some articles making the case for the efficiencies to be gained, including the following; https://hbr.org/2014/09/the-economic-advantages-of-an-independent-scotland

4   Future life expectancy in 35 industrialised countries: projections with a Bayesian model ensemble, Kontis, Vasilis et al., *The Lancet*, Volume 389 , Issue 10076 , 1323 – 1335.

5   March of the machines: A special report on Artificial Intelligence, The Economist, June 25th-July 1st 2016.

Chapter 3

1   How great leaders inspire action by Simon Sinek has now amassed

more than 37 million views on the TED site: https://www.ted.com/talks/simon_sinek_how_great_leaders_inspire_action

2   Seneca the Younger was one of the main Stoic philosophers, a school of thought that we touch on several times throughout the book. The Roman Emperor Marcus Aurelius was another well-known proponent of Stoicism.

3   *Rosenthal, Robert; Jacobson, Lenore (1992). Pygmalion in the classroom : teacher expectation and pupils' intellectual development (Newly expanded ed.). Bancyfelin, Carmarthen, Wales: Crown House Pub. ISBN 978-1904424062.*

Chapter 4

1   https://www.ons.gov.uk/peoplepopulationandcommunity/wellbeing/articles/measuring-nationalwellbeing/apr2017

2   An Inquiry into the Nature and Causes of the Wealth of Nations, Adam Smith, Originally published March 1776.

3   Creating Sustainable Performance, Gretchen Spreitzer and Christine Porath, Harvard Business Review, Jan-Feb 2012.

4   Flow: The Psychology of Optimal Experience, Mihály Csíkszentmihályi, Harper Perennial Modern Classics, 2008.

5   An interesting application of managing employees using Flow states is provided on First Round Review here: http://firstround.

com/review/track-and-facilitate-your-engineers-flow-states-in-this-simple-way/ In addition to the usual Flow categories they discuss the extreme states of Apathy = Low Skill and Low Challenge, Anxiety = Low Skill and High Challenge, and Boredom = High Skill and Low Challenge. Transitionary states are Doubt when moving from Flow towards Anxiety, and Nostalgia when moving from Flow towards Boredom.

6   The Rand workplace wellness programs study by Soeren Mattke and colleagues can be downloaded at the following link: https://www.rand.org/pubs/research_reports/RR254.html

7   A Harvard Business Review interview with Andre Spicer, one of the authors of *The Wellness Syndrome* can be found here: https://hbr.org/2015/05/corporate-wellness-programs-make-us-unwell

8   Mindfulness can literally change your brain, Christina Congleton, Britta K. Hölzel and Sara W. Lazar, Harvard Business Review Blog, 8th January 2015. Available online at: https://hbr.org/2015/01/mind-fulness-can-literally-change-your-brain

9   S. Danziger, J. Levav, and L. Avnaim-Pesso, "Extraneous Factors in Judicial Deci- sions," *PNAS (Proceedings of the National Academy of Sciences of the United States of America)* vol. 108, no. 17 (April 26, 2011): 6889–6892.

Chapter 5

1　Many books have been written on the exploits of the explorer Ernest Henry Shackleton. For a concise and specific treatment of leadership we recommend the Harvard Business School Case 803-127: Leadership in Crisis: Ernest Shackleton and the Epic Voyage of the Endurance, by Nancy F. Koehn, Erica Helms and Philip Mead, April 2003.

Chapter 6

1　The New York Times magazine included a story on the rise and fall of Amy Cuddy on October 18th 2017, which gives great insight into the merging of science and celebrity in the Internet age: *When the Revolution Came for Amy Cuddy,* by Susan Dominus. Available online at: https://www.nytimes.com/2017/10/18/magazine/when-the-revolution-came-for-amy-cuddy.html

2　What the Body Tells Us about Leadership by Art Kleiner, strategy+business, August 7th 2017. Available online at: https://www.strategy-business.com/article/What-the-Body-Tells-Us-about-Leadership

3　See Take Off, Reference (2)

4　N. Merchant, "Sitting Is the Smoking of Our Generation," HBR Blog (January 14, 2013). https://hbr.org/2013/01/sitting-is-the-smoking-of-our-generation/.

5　"Calorie burner: How much better is standing up than sitting?" *BBC News Magazine* (October 16, 2013). http://www.bbc.co.uk/news/magazine-24532996.

6　M. Oppezzo and D. L. Schwartz, "Give Your Ideas Some Legs: The Positive Effect of Walking on Creative Thinking," *Journal of Experimental Psychology: Learning, Memory, and Cognition* vol. 40, no. 4 (2014): 1142–1152

7　Kandola A, Hendrikse J, Lucassen PJ, Yücel M. Aerobic Exercise as a Tool to Improve Hippocampal Plasticity and Function in Humans: Practical Implications for Mental Health Treatment. Front Hum Neurosci. 2016;10:373.

8　Cassilhas RC, Tufik S, de Mello MT. Physical exercise, neuroplasticity, spatial learning and memory. Cell Mol Life Sci. 2016;73(5):975-83.

9　Bherer L. Cognitive plasticity in older adults: effects of cognitive training and physical exercise. Ann N Y Acad Sci. 2015;1337:1-6.

10　Heijnen S, Hommel B, Kibele A, Colzato LS. Neuromodulation of Aerobic Exercise-A Review. Front Psychol. 2016;6:1890.

Chapter 7

1　Diffusion of Innovations (5th edition) Everett M. Rogers, Free Press.

2　Innovation: The Attacker's Advantage, Richard Foster, Summit Books.

Chapter 8

1 Work/life integration? No, thanks – I'd rather have balance, Ruth Whippman, The Pool. Available online at: https://www.the-pool.com/work/work-smarter/2017/17/ruth-whippman-on-work-life-balance

2 A new perspective: Chrono-biochemistry, H. W. Simpson, Essays in Medical Biochemistry II, (1976) 2, 115-187.

3 Diurnal and Seasonal Mood Vary with Work, Sleep, and Daylength Across Diverse Cultures, SCOTT A. GOLDER, MICHAEL W. MACY, *SCIENCE*, 30 SEP 2011: 1878-1881.

4 Circadian Entrainment to the Natural Light-Dark Cycle across Seasons and the Weekend, Stothard, Ellen R. et al., Current Biology, Volume 27 , Issue 4 , 508 – 513.

5 Most of Professor Shiv's work on Serotonin and Leadership comes within the context of his X framework. A good starting point for this would be the following article published on the Stranford Graduate School of Business website in 2013: https://www.gsb.stanford.edu/insights/baba-shiv-how-do-you-find-breakthrough-ideas

6 An Internet meme showing the result of this hormone balance went viral in 2016. Love, happiness, and anxiety were some of the states shown for corresponding levels of Dopamine, Serotonin, and Oxytocin. While not completely accurate it shows the impact these chemicals have on our day-to-day mood and wellbeing: https://imgur.com/gallery/G624q

Chapter 9

1 Tamara Carleton and William Cockayne summarized much of their industry experience in *The Playbook for Strategic Foresight and Innovation* a free resource which can be downloaded at the Stanford University Foresight and Innovation lab here: https://foresight.stanford.edu

2 The original interview with Jose Maria was published in the Sustaining Executive Performance book (Take Off, Ref 2). The transcript of the interview was published for the first time on the Blog of The Leadership Academy of Barcelona, available here: http://www.thelabcn.com/blog/2016/3/13/an-interview

3 *The Practice of Adaptive Leadership: Tools and Tactics for Changing Your Organization and the World*, Ronald Heifetz, Alexander Grashow and Marty Linsky, Harvard Business Review Press, 2009.

Chapter 10

1 *Thinking, Fast and Slow*, Daniel Kahneman, Farrar, Straus and Giroux, 2013.

2 Lally et al. How are habits formed: Modelling habit formation in the real world, European Journal of Social Psychology, 2010

3 See Chapter 9, Reference 2.

4   *How Google Optimized Healthy Office Snacks*, by Zoe Chance, Ravi Dhar, Michelle Hatzis and Michiel Bakker, Harvard Business Review Blog, 3rd March 2016. Available online at: https://hbr.org/2016/03/how-google-uses-behavioral-economics-to-make-its-employees-healthier

5   *Want to be More Productive? Sit Next to Someone Who Is*, by Jason Corsello and Dylan Minor, Harvard Business Review Blog, 14th February 2017. Available online at: https://hbr.org/2017/02/want-to-be-more-productive-sit-next-to-someone-who-is

6   *Here comes SuperBoss*, Schumpeter on The Economist, December 16th 2015.

7   For the 2016 dataset all core program attendees at Telefónica University (around 1900) attended a Sustaining Executive Performance course. In short sessions spread over 3 days content was delivered on the 'WHAT' of executive health including mobility and exercise, sleep, mindfulness and nutrition and the 'HOW' of making good intentions stick with basic instruction on successful behaviour change. At the end of their course they wrote a self-addressed letter outlining a new positive habit that would improve their health and performance. This letter was mailed to them 100 days after the end of their course. On the letter was a link to an online form with two questions. An e-mail reminder was then sent to all to complete the questions.

The first question asked the degree of success on a scale from 1 to 5, where 1 was having "completely forgotten about the commitment until the letter arrived" and 5 having "a new automatic daily habit." The second question asked the respondent to choose from a list of 4 choices on where and when the habit was placed; 1) in the morning before arriving at work, 2) in the morning at work, 3) at work after lunch, and 4) in the evening after leaving work. We achieved a response rate over 30% and a total of 574 answers.

Our questions were designed to gain insight into two key variables for habit formation success; the environment and the time of day. Although we didn't have well-formed hypotheses prior to the study we did have some expectations based on other research in the field as well as our own leadership development experiences the past 10 years. For example, regarding the time of day variable 'decision fatigue' research has found decision making to worsen as the day has proceeded. Other studies have shown both the likliehood to follow rules and even ethics to decrease over the course of time. Our expectation was therefore that the most successful habits would have been placed in the morning.

The importance of the environment, in our case either home

or work, also provided an interesting variable, and connects with the SURROUNDINGS element of the 7S model. We would expect the home environment to be more 'designed', that is, shaped proactively by the respondent. Whether such changes would support good or bad habits is however open to question. The work environment design in contrast would be more outwith their control though it may offer greater discipline to follow through with habits in the health domain. In any case our expectation was that the home environment would offer a better opportunity for habit formation success, also because they would be more focused on their personal lives with healthy habits still perceived by many as a non-work topic.

For the 2017 dataset all attendees (around 1300) attended short sessions but this time with a greater focus on understanding habits. A total of two 45 minute sessions called 'Habit Hacking' were delivered within the usual weekly format of programs at the University. A commitment to one habit, either a new positive one to be implemented or an existing negative one to stop, was made at the end of the second session and shared directly with us via an online form. We then e-mailed back this change commitment 100 days after their attendance at the University and asked them how successful they were, again using a Likert 5 point scale, together with the identification of which of the seven habit 'hacks' they employed (with the 7S model having been presented in class). We also asked them the one key determining factor in their success or failure.

8 Big Data and Tourism: New Indicators for Tourism Management, A publication by RocaSalvatella and Telefonica, May 2014.

Chapter 11

1 Some employees are rumored to hate the open floor plan at Apple's new $5 billion campus, Kif Leswing, Business Insider, August 7th 2017. http://www.businessinsider.com/apple-employees-rumored-hate-apple-park-open-floor-plan-2017-8

2 Global Impact of Biophilic Design in the Workplace, A Human Spaces report by Interface and led by Professor Sir Cary Cooper.

3 A summary of this research, carried out at the University of Exeter can be found here: http://www.exeter.ac.uk/news/research/title_306119_en.html

4 https://www.wellcertified.com

Chapter 12

1 We interviewed Professor Barnes for the book and have started to collaborate on new research projects. A summary of his recent research can be found on his faculty page here: https://foster.uw.edu/faculty-research/directory/christopher-barnes/

2 Age effects in perception of time, Wittmann M., Lehnhoff S. Psychol Rep. 2005 Dec;97(3):921-35.

Sharing knowledge since 1993